The New Gods

E. M. Cioran:

The New Gods

TRANSLATED FROM
THE FRENCH BY
RICHARD HOWARD
QUADRANGLE/
THE NEW YORK TIMES
BOOK CO.

LIBRARY OF CONGRESS CATALOGING IN PUBLICATION DATA

Cioran, Émile M   1911–
  The new gods.

  Translation of Le Mauvais démiurge.
  1. Creation. 2. Good and evil. 3. Man (Theology)
4. Suicide. I. Title.
BL226.C5613   210   74-77939
ISBN 0-8129-0475-3

The New Gods

THE DEMIURGE

WITH THE EXCEPTION of some aberrant cases, man does not incline to the good: what god would impel him to do so? Man must vanquish himself, must do himself violence, in order to perform the slightest action untainted by evil. And each time he succeeds, he provokes or humiliates his Creator. If he manages to be good—no longer by effort or calculation, but by nature—he owes his achievement to an inadvertence from on high: he situates himself outside the universal order; he was foreseen by no divine plan. It is difficult to say what station the good man occupies among what we call *beings*, even if he is one. Perhaps he is a ghost?

The good is what was or will be—it is what never *is*. Parasite of memory or of anticipation, past or possible, it cannot be *actual*—present—nor subsist in and of itself: as such, consciousness knows it not, and apprehends it only when it disappears. Everything proves its insubstantiality; the good is a great, unreal force, a principle which has miscarried from the start: lapse, immemorial failure, its effects are accentuated with the course of history. In the beginning, in that primal promiscuity where the swerve toward life occurred, something unspeakable must have happened which continues in our discomforts, if not in our reasonings. Who could help concluding that existence has been vitiated at its source, existence and the elements themselves? The man who fails to envisage this hypothesis at least once a day has gone through life as a sleep-walker.

*

It is difficult, it is impossible to believe that the Good Lord —"Our Father"—had a hand in the scandal of creation. Everything suggests that He took no part in it, that it proceeds from a god without scruples, a feculent god. Goodness does not create, lacking imagination; it takes imagination to put together a world, however botched. At the very least, there must be a mixture of good and evil in order to produce an action or a work. Or a universe. Considering ours, it is altogether easier to trace matters back to a suspect god than to an honorable one.

The Good Lord was certainly not equipped for creating: He possesses everything except omnipotence. Great by His weaknesses (anemia and kindness are partners), He is the prototype of ineffectuality: He can help no one. . . . Moreover, we cling to Him only when we cast off our historical dimension; as soon as we resume it, He is alien to us, incomprehensible: He has nothing which fascinates us, nothing of the monster. Whereupon we turn to the creator, inferior and officious god, instigator of events. In order to understand how he could have created, we must imagine him at grips with evil, which is innovation, and with good, which is inertia. This struggle must have been fatal to evil, which was thereby obliged to endure the contamination of good—thus, the creation could not be altogether wicked.

Since evil presides over all that is corruptible, in other words over all that is alive, it is absurd to try to prove it comprises less being than good does, or even that it contains none at all. Those who identify evil with nothingness suppose they are thereby *saving* their poor Good Lord. We save Him only if we have the courage to sever His cause from that of the

Demiurge. Having refused to do so, Christianity inveterately sought to impose the inevidence of a merciful Creator: a hopeless enterprise which has exhausted Christianity and compromised the God it sought to preserve.

We cannot help thinking that the Creation, had it remained *in the rough*, neither could be completed nor deserved to be; the Creation is in fact a *fault*, man's famous sin thereby appearing as a minor version of a much graver one. What are we guilty of, except of having followed, more or less slavishly, the Creator's example? Easy to recognize in ourselves the fatality which was His: not for nothing have we issued from the hands of a wicked and woebegone god, a god accursed.

*

Some doomed to believe in the supreme but impotent God, others in the Demiurge, still others in the Devil, we choose neither our venerations nor our blasphemies.

The Devil is the representative, the delegate of the Demiurge, whose affairs he manages here on earth. Despite his prestige and the terror attached to his name, he is merely an administrator, merely an angel assigned to a menial task—to history.

Quite different is the sway of the Demiurge: how, in his absence, would we face our ordeals? If we were equal to them, or even worthy of them to some degree, we could abstain from invoking him. Before our evident inadequacies, we cling to him, we even beg him to exist: if he were to turn out to be a fiction, conceive our distress, our shame! Upon whom else would we vent our failures, our miseries, ourselves? Appointed by our fiat the author of our deficiencies, he serves as our excuse for all we cannot be. When furthermore we make him assume the responsibility for this defective universe, we enjoy a certain peace: no more uncertainty about our origins or our prospects, but the utmost security in the insoluble, outside the nightmare of promises. His merit is indeed inestimable:

indeed he releases us from our regrets, since he has taken upon himself even the *initiative* of our defeats.

It is more important to recover, in divinity, our vices than our virtues. We are resigned to our qualities, whereas our defects pursue us, torment us. What a comfort, what a reassurance to be able to project them into a god susceptible of falling to our level, a god not confined in the insipidity of commonly acknowledged attributes. The Demiurge is the most *useful* god who ever was. If he were not under our hand, where would our bile be poured out? Each and every form of hate tends as a last resort toward him. Since we all believe that our merits are misunderstood or flouted, how admit that so general an iniquity could be the doing of mere man? It must go back further and belong to some ancient dirty work, to the very act of the Creation. Thus we know whom to blame, whom to disparage: nothing flatters and sustains us so much as being able to put the source of our indignity as far away from us as possible.

As for God in the strict sense, the good and debilitated One, we come to terms with Him whenever there no longer remains in us the trace of a world, in those moments that postulate Him, those moments that, attached to Him from the start, provoke Him, *create* Him, and during which He ascends from our depths for the greatest humiliation of our gibes. God is the grief of irony. Yet let our sarcasms get a hold of themselves, let them regain the upper hand, and our relations with Him are strained and broken. Then we tire of questioning ourselves on His account, we want to dismiss Him from our preoccupations and our passions, even from our contempt. So many others before us have dealt Him telling blows that it seems futile to come now and pummel a corpse. And yet He still counts for us, if only by our regret at not having trounced Him ourselves.

*

In order to evade the difficulties inherent in dualism, we might postulate a single God whose history would develop in two phases: in the first, discreet, anemic, retiring, with no impulse to manifest Himself, a sleeping God exhausted by His own eternity; in the second phase, ambitious, frenzied, a God committing mistake after mistake, participating in a supremely blameworthy activity. Upon reflection, this hypothesis seems less clear-cut and less advantageous than that of the two distinct gods. But if we find that neither one accounts for what this world is worth, we shall then always have the resource of believing, with certain Gnostics, that it was drawn by lot among the angels.

(It is pitiable, it is degrading to identify the divinity with a person. Divinity will never be an idea nor an anonymous principle for the man who has frequented the Testaments. Twenty centuries of altercation are not forgotten overnight. Whether taking its inspiration from Job or from Saint Paul, our religious life is dispute, outrage, excess. Atheists, so ready with their invective, prove that they have *someone* in their sights. They should be less conceited; their emancipation is not so complete as they suppose: they have exactly the same notion of God as believers.)

*

The Creator is the absolute of external man; the inner man, in return, considers the Creation as an awkward detail, as a futile episode, even a fatal one. Every profound religious experience begins precisely where the realm of the Demiurge ends. It has only him to deal with—it denounces him, it is his negation. So much does he obsess us, he and the world, that there is no way of escaping either, in order to unite, in an outburst of annihilation, with the uncreated and to dissolve within it.

With the help of ecstasy, whose object is a god *without attributes*, an *essence* of god, we raise ourselves toward a purer form of apathy than that of the supreme God Himself, and if we plunge into the divine, we are nonetheless beyond any form of divinity for that. Here is the final stage, the goal of mysticism; the point of departure being the break with the Demiurge, the refusal to consort further with him and to applaud his works. No one kneels to him; no one venerates him. The only words we address to the Demiurge are backward supplications—sole mode of communication between an equally fallen creature and creator.

*

By inflicting upon the official God the functions of Father, Creator and general manager, we exposed Him to attacks to which He was to succumb. What might have been His longevity if only we had heeded Marcion, of all heresiarchs the one who most vigorously opposed evil's sleight of hand, who contributed most to the glory of the Demiurge by the hatred he felt for him! There is no example of another religion which, at the outset, has missed so many opportunities. We should assuredly be quite different if the Christian era had been inaugurated by the execration of the Creator, for the permission to abuse Him would not have failed to lighten our burden, and to render the last two millennia that much less oppressive. By refusing to incriminate Him and to adopt the doctrines which would unhesitatingly do so, the Church was to commit itself to cunning and deception. At least we have the comfort of observing that what is most alluring in its history are its most intimate enemies, all those it has opposed and rejected, those who, in order to safeguard God's honor, impugned—at the risk of martyrdom—His role as Creator. Fanatics of the divine nothingness, of that absence in which the Supreme Good delights, they knew the joy of hating this God and of loving that one without restrictions, without second thoughts. Swept on by their faith, they would have been in no position to discern the touch of imposture which enters into even the sincerest torment. The notion of *pretext* was not yet born, nor was that quite modern temptation of hiding our agonies behind some theological acrobatics.

Yet a certain ambiguity existed among them: what were these Gnostics and these Manicheans of every sort but *perverts* of purity, compulsives of horror? Evil attracted them, almost overwhelmed them: without evil, their existence would have been . . . vacant. They hunted it down, unflagging. And if they argued so vehemently that evil was *uncreated*, it was because they secretly longed for it to subsist forever, in order that they might delight in it, might practice, through all eternity, their combative virtues. Having, for love of the Father, reflected to excess upon the Adversary, they were to end by understanding damnation better than salvation. This is why they had grasped so well the essence of the fallen world. Will the Church, after having spewed them forth, be clever enough to appropriate their theses, and charitable enough to cast the Creator in a starring role in order to excommunicate Him at the end? It will be reborn only by exhuming the heresies, by annulling its old anathemas in order to pronounce new ones.

*

Timid, devoid of dynamism, the good is inept at communicating itself. Evil, much more zealous, seeks to transmit itself, and succeeds because it possesses the double privilege of being fascinating and contagious. Hence we see a bad Demiurge extend himself, get outside himself more easily than a good God.

We have all inherited something of this incapacity to remain within ourselves, whereof the Creator was to make so vexing a demonstration: *to engender* is to continue in another fashion and on another scale the enterprise which bears his name—it is, by a deplorable mimicry, to add to His "creation." Without the encouragement He has given, the desire to extend

the chain of beings would not exist, nor that necessity to subscribe to the gimmicks of the flesh. Every childbirth is suspect: the angels, luckily, are unsuited to it, the propagation
of life being reserved to the fallen. The plague is impatient
and greedy; it loves to spread. There is every reason to dis-
courage generation, for the fear of seeing humanity die out
has no basis: whatever happens, there will everywhere be
enough fools who ask only to perpetuate themselves, and, if
they themselves end by flinching from the task, there will
always be found, to devote themselves to the cause, some
hideous couple . . . .

It is not so much the appetite for life that is to be opposed
as the lust for lineage. Parents—*genitors*—are provocateurs or
mad. What could be more demoralizing than the fact that the
worst freak should have the faculty of giving life, of "bringing
into the world?" How contemplate without dread or repulsion
the wonder that makes the first man in the street a demiurge
on the brink? What should be a gift as exceptional as genius
has been conferred indiscriminately upon all: a liberality of
base coinage which forever disqualifies nature.

The criminal injunction of Genesis—"Be fruitful and multiply . . ."—could never have come out of the mouth of the
Good Lord. *"Be ye rare,"* He would have suggested, surely, if
He had had any say in the matter. Nor could He ever have
added the fatal words: ". . . and replenish the earth." They
should be erased without delay, in order to cleanse the Bible
of the shame of having garnered them.

The flesh spreads, further and further, like a gangrene upon
the surface of the globe. It cannot impose limits upon itself,
it continues to be rife despite its rebuffs, it takes its defeats
for conquests, it has never learned anything. It belongs above
all to the realm of the Creator, and it is indeed in the flesh
that He has projected His maleficent instincts. Normally, the
flesh should be less harmful to those who contemplate it than
to those who extend its duration and assure its progress. Far

from it, for they do not know what aberration it is that they are accomplices of. Pregnant women will some day be stoned to death, the maternal instinct proscribed, sterility acclaimed. It is with good reason that in the sects which held fecundity in suspicion—the Bogomils, for instance, and the Cathari—marriage was condemned; that abominable institution which all societies have always protected, to the despair of those who do not yield to the common delirium. To procreate is to love the scourge—to seek to maintain and to augment it. They were right, those ancient philosophers who identified fire with the principle of the universe, and with desire, for desire burns, devours, annihilates: At once agent and destroyer of beings, it is sombre, it is infernal by essence.

This world was not created in joy. Yet we *pro*create in pleasure. True enough—but pleasure is not joy, it is joy's simulacrum: its function consists in deceiving, in making us forget that creation bears, down to its least detail, the mark of that initial melancholy from which it issued. Necessarily illusory, it is pleasure too which permits us to carry out certain performances which in theory we repudiate. Without its cooperation, continence, gaining ground, would seduce even the rats. But it is in what we call the transports of the flesh that we understand how fraudulent pleasure is. In the flesh, pleasure reaches its peak, its maximum intensity, and it is here, at the zenith of its success, that it suddenly opens to its unreality, that it collapses in its own void. The voluptuous flesh is the *disaster* of pleasure.

We cannot grant that a god, *or even a man*, proceeds from a gymnastic climaxed by a moan. It is curious that at the end of such a long period of time, "evolution" has not managed to perfect another formula. Why should it take the trouble, moreover, when the one in force functions so well and suits everybody? Let there be no mistake: life in itself is not in question, life is as mysterious and enervating as could be wished. What is not so is the exercise in question, of an inadmissible facility, *given the consequences.* When we know what fate permits each man, we remain stunned by the disproportion between a moment's oblivion and the prodigious quantity of disgraces which result from it. The more one reverts to this subject, the more one finds that the only men who have understood anything about it are those who have opted for orgy or for asceticism, the debauched or the castrated.

Since procreation supposes a nameless distraction, it is certain that if we were to become prudent, in other words indifferent to the fate of the race, we should retain only a few samples, the way we preserve certain creatures of vanishing species. Let us block the way of all flesh, let us try to paralyze its alarming spread. We are in the presence of a veritable epidemic of life, a proliferation of faces. Where and how to remain, still, face-to-face with God?

No one is continually subject to the obsession with this horror. Sometimes we turn from it, almost forget it, especially when we contemplate some landscape from which our own kind is absent. Once they appear there, the obsession returns, settles down in the mind. If we were inclined to absolve the creator, to consider this world as acceptable and even satisfying, we should still have to make certain reservations about man, that blot on the creation.

*

We can imagine that the Demiurge, imbued with the inadequacy or the harmfulness of his production, might someday cause it to perish, and even manage to disappear along with it. But we can also conceive that down through the ages he has been concerned only to destroy himself and that what we call becoming is no more than the slow process of this autodestruction. Lagging or gasping, in either eventuality the process involves a reflexive movement, a scrutiny of conscience, whose result would be the casting out of the creation by its author.

What is anchored deepest in us and is least perceptible is the sentiment of an essential failure, hidden from all, including the gods. And what is remarkable is that most of us are far from realizing that we experience this sentiment. We are, moreover, by a special favor of nature, doomed not to become aware of it: Our power resides in our incapacity to know how alone we are. Blessed ignorance, thanks to which we can act, or at least act up. Once we have the revelation of this secret, our inner spring immediately breaks, and irremediably. This is what has happened to the Creator, or what will happen to Him, perhaps.

*

Always to have lived with the nostalgia to coincide with something, but not really knowing with what . . . . It is easy to shift from unbelief to belief, or conversely. But what is there to convert to, and what is there to abjure, in a state of chronic lucidity? Lacking substance, it offers no content that can be disclaimed; it is empty, and one does not disclaim the void: lucidity is the negative equivalent of ecstasy.

To coincide with nothing is not to coincide any better with ourselves; whence these faithless appeals, these vacillating convictions, these fervor-lacking fevers, this division which makes a victim of our ideas and even of our reflexes. At first we kept that ambiguity which governs all our relations with this world and the other for ourselves. Subsequently we have extended it around us, so that no one may escape it, so that no man alive knows what he may still abide by. Nothing *clear* anywhere: By our defection, things themselves stagger and subside into perplexity. What we need is that gift of imagining the possibility of prayer, indispensable to anyone in pursuit of his salvation. Hell is *inconceivable* prayer.

The founding of a universal ambiguity is our most calamitous exploit—it makes us rivals of the Demiurge.

*

We were happy only in the ages when, greedy for obliteration, we enthusiastically accepted our nothingness. Religious feeling emanates not from the acknowledgement of but from the desire for our insignificance, from our need to wallow in it. How will this need, inherent in our nature, be satisfied now that we can no longer live in the wake of the gods? In other times it was the gods who abandoned us; today we abandon them. We have lived beside them too long for them still to find grace in our sight. Always within reach, we heard them stirring; they watched us, spied on us: we were no longer at home. Now, as experience teaches, there exists no being more odious than our neighbor. The fact of knowing him to be so close in space keeps us from breathing and makes our days and our nights equally unfeasible. Try as we will to brood upon his ruin, he is there, hideously present. To suppress him is the impulse of every thought; when we finally determine to do so, a spasm of cowardice grips us, just before the act. Thus, we are the potential murderers of those who live beside us; and from our incapacity to be the actual ones comes our torment, our bitterness, dilettantes and eunuchs of bloodshed that we are.

If, with the gods, everything seemed simpler, it is because their indiscretion was immemorial. We had to be done with it at all costs: Were they not too cumbersome to be endured any longer? Hence none of us could fail to add his little voice to the general hue and cry against them.

When we think of these age-old companions or enemies, of all the lords of sects, religions and mythologies, the only one we are reluctant to part with is this Demiurge, to whom we attach the very evils we so much want him to be the cause of. It is the Demiurge we think of apropos of each and every act of life and of life itself. Whenever we consider it, whenever we examine its origins, life amazes us, alarms us; it is a dreadful miracle which must proceed from *him*, a special god, a case utterly apart. There is no use insisting he does not exist, when our daily stupors are there to demand his reality and to proclaim it. Even if we argue that perhaps he existed but that he has died like the rest, those stupors of ours will not be gainsaid. They will busy themselves reviving him, and he will last as long as our amazement and our alarm, as long as our intimidated curiosity before all that is, all that lives. We may say: "Conquer fear, so that only amazement remains." But to conquer fear, to make it vanish, we should have to attack its very principle and demolish its foundations, to rebuild nothing more or less than the world in its totality, nimbly to switch Demiurges, confiding ourselves, in short, to *another* creator.

THE NEW GODS

A MAN INTERESTED in the procession of ideas and of irreducible beliefs will find it worth his while to pause over the spectacle afforded by the first centuries of our era: here he will discover the very model of all the forms of conflict to be met with, in attenuated form, at any moment of history. Quite understandably: this is the epoch when men hated the most. For which the credit goes to the Christians, feverish, intractable, from the start expert in the art of detestation; whereas the pagans could no longer manage anything but scorn. Aggression is a trait common to men and new gods.

If some monster of amenity, ignorant of spleen, nonetheless wanted to become versed in that subject, or at least to learn what it is worth, the simplest method would be for him to read some ecclesiastical authors, beginning with Tertullian, the most brilliant of all, and ending, say, with Saint Gregory of Nazianzus, rancorous yet insipid, whose oration against Julian the Apostate makes you feel like converting then and there to paganism. The emperor is conceded no virtues whatever; with unconcealed satisfaction, his heroic death in the Persian War is contested, for Gregory claims he was despatched by "a barbarian who was a buffoon by trade, following the armies in order to divert the soldiers from the hardships of war by his gibes and witticisms." No elegance, no concern to appear worthy of such an adversary. What is un-forgivable in the saint's case is that he had known Julian at Athens, in the days when the two young men had frequented the philosophical schools there.

Nothing more odious than the tone of those who are de-fending a cause, one compromised in appearance, winning in fact; who cannot contain their delight at the idea of their triumph nor help turning their very terrors into so many threats. When Tertullian, sardonic and trembling, describes the Last Judgment, "the greatest of spectacles," as he calls it, he imagines the laugh he will have contemplating so many monarchs and gods "uttering dreadful groans in the depths of the abyss. . . ." This insistence upon reminding the pagans that they were lost, they and their idols, was liable to exasperate even the most temperate. A series of libels camou-flaged as treatises, Christian apologetics represents the acme of the bilious genre.

Man can breathe only in the shadow of eroded divinities. The more convinced of this we are, the more we remind our-selves, in terror, that had we lived at the moment of Chris-tianity's rise, we might well have submitted to its fascination. The beginnings of a religion (like the beginnings of anything) are always suspect. They alone, though, possess some reality, they alone are *true*; true and abominable. We do not watch the founding of a god, whoever he may be and wherever he comes from, with impunity. Nor is this disadvantage a recent one: Prometheus already called attention to it, a victim to Zeus and the new gang of Olympus.

Much more than the prospect of salvation, it was rage against the ancient world which swept on the Christians in a single impulse of destruction. Since they came for the most part from elsewhere, their outburst of fury against Rome is understandable. But what sort of frenzy was it in which the citizen participated when he became a convert? Not so well prepared as the others, he possessed but one recourse: to hate himself. Without this deviation of hatred, at first atypical, subsequently contagious, Christianity would have remained no more than a sect, limited to a foreign clientele, actually capable of no more than painlessly trading in the old gods for a nailed corpse. Let the man who wonders how he would have reacted to Constantine's change of policy put himself in the place of a partisan of the tradition, a pagan proud of being so: how consent to the Cross, how tolerate that symbol of a disgraceful death emblazoned on the Roman standards? Yet such men resigned themselves to it, and it is difficult for us to imagine the cumulus of inner defeats from which this resignation issued. If, in the moral realm, we may conceive it as the consummation of a crisis, and thereby grant it the status or the excuse of a conversion, such resignation appears as a betrayal as soon as we consider it from the political viewpoint. To abandon the gods who made Rome was to abandon Rome herself, to form an alliance with this "new race of men born yesterday, having neither country nor traditions, leagued together against every religious and civil institution, pursued by the law, universally decried for their infamies, yet glorying in this common execration." Celsius's diatribe dates from 178. About two centuries later, Julian was to write, "If, in the reigns of Tiberius or Claudius, a single distinguished mind is known to have become a convert to Christian ideas, consider me as the greatest of impostors."

The "new race of men" was to take no end of trouble before overcoming the scruples of the cultivated. How trust these unknown men who were appearing out of the lower depths and whose every gesture invited disdain? For that was just it: by what means accept the God of those one despises and Who was furthermore of such recent manufacture? Age alone guaranteed the validity of the gods—all were tolerated, provided they were not newly minted. What was regarded as particularly troublesome in the case was the absolute novelty of the Son: a contemporary, a parvenu. . . . It was this disheartening figure whom no *sage* had foreseen nor pre-figured, who "shocked" most. His appearance was a scandal which it took four centuries to get used to. The Father, an old acquaintance, was admitted; for tactical reasons the Christians fell back upon Him and spoke in His name: were not the books which celebrated Him and whose spirit the Gospels perpetuated, according to Tertullian, several centuries older than the temples, the oracles, the pagan gods? The apologist, once launched, goes so far as to claim that Moses antedates the fall of Troy by several thousand years. Such divagations were meant to combat the effect which might be provoked by remarks like this of Celsius's: "After all, the Jews, many centuries ago, organized themselves into a nation, established laws of their own which they retain even today. The religion they observe, whatever its worth and whatever may be said of it, is the religion of their ancestors. By remaining faithful to it, they do no more than other men do as well, who all preserve the customs of their country."

To sacrifice to the prejudice of antiquity was implicitly to recognize the indigenous gods as the only legitimate ones. The Christians were quite willing, for selfish motives, to bow to this prejudice as such, but they could not, without destroying themselves, go further and adopt it entirely, with all its consequences. For an Origen, the ethnic gods were idols, relics of polytheism; Saint Paul had already reduced them to the rank of demons. Judaism regarded them all as false except one, its own. "Their only error," Julian says of the Jews, "is that even as they seek to satisfy their god, they do not serve the others at the same time." Yet he praises them for their repugnance to follow the fashion with regard to religion. "I shun innovation in all things, and especially in that which concerns the gods"—an admission which has discredited him and which is used to brand him as a "reactionary." But what "progress," one wonders, does Christianity represent in relation to paganism? There is no "qualitative leap" from one god to another, nor from one civilization to another, any more than from one language to another. Who would dare to proclaim the superiority of the Christian writers over the pagan ones? Even the Prophets, though of another inspiration and another style than the Church Fathers, produced, Saint Jerome confesses, an aversion in the reader who has returned to Cicero or to Plautus. "Progress" at the time was embodied in these unreadable Fathers: then, was to turn away from them to go over to "reaction"? Julian was entirely correct in preferring to them Homer, Thucydides, or Plato. The edict by which he forbade Christian educators to explicate the Greek authors has been harshly criticized, not only by his adversaries but even by all his admirers, in all periods. Without seeking to justify him, one cannot help understanding him. He was dealing with fanatics; to gain their respect it was occasionally necessary to exaggerate as they did, to spin out some nonsense for their sake, or else they would have scorned him as no more than an amateur. He therefore requires these "instructors" to imitate the writers they were expounding and to share their opinions of the gods. "Yet if they believe that these authors have been deceived as to the most important point, let them go into the churches of the Galileans to offer commentaries on Matthew and Luke!"

In the eyes of the ancients, the more gods you recognize, the better you serve divinity, whereof they are but the aspects, the faces. To seek to limit their number was an impiety; to suppress them all for the sake of but one, a crime. It is of this crime that the Christians made themselves guilty. Irony in their regard was no longer appropriate: The evil they were propagating had gained too much ground. All of Julian's harshness derives from the impossibility of treating them offhandedly.

*

Polytheism corresponds better to the diversity of our tendencies and our impulses, which it offers the possibility of expressing, of manifesting; each of them being free to tend, according to its nature, toward the god who suits it at the moment. But how deal with a single god? How envisage him, how *utilize* him? In his presence, we live continually under pressure. Monotheism curbs our sensibility: it deepens us by narrowing us. A system of constraints which affords us an inner dimension at the cost of the flowering of our powers, it constitutes a barrier, it halts our expansion, it throws us out of gear. Surely we were more normal with several gods than we are with only one. If *health* is a criterion, what a setback monotheism turns out to be!

Under the regime of several gods, fervor is shared. When it is addressed to one god alone it is concentrated, exacerbated, and ends by turning into aggression, into *faith*. Energy is no longer dispersed, it is entirely focussed in one direction. What was remarkable in paganism is that no radical distinction was made between believing and not believing, having faith or not having it. Faith is a Christian invention; it supposes one and the same disequilibrium in man and in God, swept on by a dialogue as dramatic as it is disordered. Whence the frantic character of the new religion. The old one, so much more human, left you the faculty of choosing the god you wanted; since it imposed none upon you, it was up to you to incline toward one or another. The more capricious you were, the more you needed to change gods, to shift from one to another, being quite certain of finding the means of adoring them all in the course of one existence. Furthermore they were modest, they demanded only respect: You hailed them, you did not kneel before them. They were ideally suited to the man whose contradictions were not resolved nor could be—to the tormented and unappeased mind. How fortunate he was, in his itinerant confusion, to be able to *try* them all and to be almost certain of falling on just the one he needed most on the occa-

sion! After the triumph of Christianity, the freedom of maneuvering among them and of choosing one to your taste became
inconceivable. Their cohabitation, their admirable promiscuity
was past. Would any esthete, wearied but not yet disgusted
with paganism, have adhered to the new religion if he had
divined that it was to spread over so many centuries? Would
he have bartered the caprice suited to a regime of interchange-
able idols for a cult whose God was to enjoy so terrifying a
longevity?

To all appearances, man has given himself gods out of a
need to be protected, guaranteed—in reality, out of a greed to
suffer. So long as man believed in a multitude of them, he had
indulged in a freedom of choice, in loopholes. Subsequently
limiting himself to just one, he was thereby afflicted by a
supplement of shackles and throes. Surely there is but one
animal which loves and hates itself to the point of vice, which
could afford the luxury of a subjection so burdensome. What
cruelty to ourselves, to join forces with the great Specter and
to weld our lot to His! *The one* God makes life unbreathable.

Christianity has made use of the Romans' juridical rigor
and the Greeks' philosophical acrobatics, not to liberate the
mind, but to enchain it. And by enchaining it, Christianity
has obliged the mind to deepen, to descend into itself. The
dogmas imprison it, assign it outer limits which it may not
exceed at any price. At the same time they leave the mind free
to explore its particular universe, to scrutinize its own vertigo,
and, in order to escape the tyranny of doctrinal certitudes, to
seek out being—or its negative equivalent—at the extreme
verge of all sensation. Experience of the pinioned mind,
ecstasy is necessarily more frequent in an authoritarian religion than in a liberal one: this is so because ecstasy is then a
leap toward the intimacy of the depths, a recourse to inwardness, *the selfward flight.*

Having had, for so long, no other refuge but God, we have
dived as deep into Him as into ourselves (a dive which repre-

mote them to the rank of victims! Everything in paganism, including toleration, exasperated them. Strong in their certainties, they could not understand *resignation* to likelihood, in the pagan manner, nor adherence to a worship whose priests, mere magistrates appointed to the perfunctory forms of ritual, imposed upon no one the burden of *sincerity*.

When we realize that life is endurable only if we can change gods, and that monotheism contains the germ of every form of tyranny, we stop commiserating with the ancient institution of slavery. It was better to be a slave and to be able to worship one's chosen deity than to be "free" and to confront only a single variety of the divine. Freedom is the right to *difference*; being plurality, it postulates the dispersion of the absolute, its resolution into a dust of truths, equally justified and provisional. There is an underlying polytheism in liberal democracy (call it an unconscious polytheism); conversely, every authoritarian regime partakes of a disguised monotheism. Curious, the effects of monotheist logic: a pagan, once he became a Christian, tended toward intolerance. Better to founder with a horde of accommodating gods than to prosper in a despot's shadow! In an age when, lacking religious conflicts, we witness ideological ones, the question raised for us is indeed the one which haunted a waning antiquity: how to renounce so many gods for just one?—with this corrective, nonetheless, that the sacrifice demanded of us is located on a lower level, no longer that of gods but that of opinions. As soon as a divinity, or a doctrine, claims supremacy, freedom is threatened. If we see a supreme value in toleration, then everything which does it violence is to be considered as a crime, starting with those enterprises of conversion in which the Church has remained unequalled. And if she has exaggerated the gravity of the persecutions she was subjected to and absurdly swelled the number of her martyrs, it is because, having been an oppressive force for so long, she needed to cover her misdeeds with noble pretexts: to leave pernicious doctrines unpunished—would this not have been a betrayal of those who had sacrificed themselves for her? Thus it was in a spirit of loyalty that the Church proceeded to the annihilation of the "strayed," and that she could, after having been persecuted for four centuries, be a persecutor for fourteen. That is the secret, the *miracle* of her perenniality. Never were martyrs avenged with more systematic tenacity.

The advent of Christianity having coincided with that of the Empire, certain Fathers (Eusebius, among others) maintained that this coincidence had a profound meaning: one God, one Emperor. In reality, it was the abolition of national barriers, the possibility of circulating throughout a vast state without frontiers, which permitted Christianity to infiltrate, to grow rampant. Without this opportunity to spread, it would have remained a simple dissidence within Judaism instead of becoming an invading religion and, what is more troublesome, a propagandizing one. All means were justified to recruit, to reinforce and to expand even those daily obsequies whose apparatus was a real offence as much for the pagans as for the Olympian gods. Julian observes that, according to the legislators of old, "since life and death differ altogether, the acts relative to one and the other must be performed separately." This disjunction the Christians, in their fanatic proselytism, were not disposed to make: they were well aware of the utility of the corpse, the advantage to be drawn from it. Paganism did not skimp death, but was careful not to put it on display. For paganism, it was a fundamental principle that death is not consonant with broad daylight, that death is an insult to the light. Death belonged to night and the infernal gods. The Galileans have filled up the sepulchers, says Julian, who never calls Jesus anything but "the dead one." For pagans worthy of the name, the new superstition could seem only an exploitation, only a harnessing of the hideous. All the more bitterly were they to deplore the progress it was making in every milieu. What Celsius could not know, but what Julian knew perfectly, were the triflers of Christianity—those who, incapable of subscribing to it altogether, nonetheless strained to follow it, fearing that if they remained apart, they would be excluded from the "future." Either from opportunism or fear of solitude, they wanted to walk beside these men "born yesterday" but soon called to the role of masters, of torturers.

*

However legitimate his passion for the defunct gods, Julian had no chance of reviving them. Instead of laboring to do so, he should have allied himself, out of fury, with the Manicheans and with them undermined the Church. By sacrificing his ideal, he would at least have satisfied his rancor. What other card than vengeance still remained in his hand? A magnificent career of demolition lay open before him, and perhaps he would have taken it up had he not been beclouded by a nostalgia for Olympus. One does not wage battles in the name of a regret. He died young, it is true—after scarcely two years of rule. With ten or twenty before him, what service would he not have rendered us all! Not that he would have smothered Christianity, but he would have compelled it to more modesty. We should be less vulnerable, for we should not have lived as if we were the center of the universe, as if everything, *even God,* revolved around us. The Incarnation is the most dangerous flattery of which we have been the object. It will have granted us an excessive status, out of all proportion with what we are. By hoisting the human anecdote to the dignity of cosmic drama, Christianity has deceived us as to our insignificance, has cast us into illusion, into that morbid optimism which, despite all the evidence, identifies progress with apotheosis. More prudently, pagan antiquity put man in his place. When Tacitus wonders if events are ruled by eternal laws or if they come about by chance, he manages to avoid answering, he leaves the question open; and this indecision nicely expresses the general feeling of the ancients. More than anyone, the historian, faced with that mixture of constants and aberrations out of which the historical process is composed, is necessarily led to oscillate between determinism and contingency, accident and law, physics and fortune. There is no misfortune which we cannot refer as we like either to a distraction of Providence or to the indifference of Chance, or finally to the inflexibility of Fate. This trinity, so conveniently applicable for anyone, especially for a disabused mind, is the most comforting thing pagan wisdom has to propose. We moderns are reluctant to resort to it, as we are no less reluctant to espouse the (specifically ancient) notion according to which blessings and misfortunes represent an invariable total which cannot undergo any modification. With our obsession with progress and regression, we implicitly admit that evil changes, either diminishes or augments. The world's identity with itself, the splendid notion that it is condemned to be what it is and that the future will add nothing essential to the existing data, no longer has any currency. This is precisely because the future, an object of horror or hope, is our true *site*; we live in it, it is everything for us. The obsession with advent, which is essentially Christian, by reducing time to the concept of the imminent and the possible, makes us ill-suited to conceive an immutable moment, resting in itself, preserved from the scourge of succession. Even stripped of the slightest content, *expectation* is a void which gratifies us, an anxiety which reassures, so unfit are we for a static vision. "There is no need for God to correct His works," an opinion of Celsius which is that of an entire civilization, runs counter to our inclinations, to our instincts, to our very being. We can ratify it only in an unwonted moment, in an outburst of wisdom. It runs counter even to what the believer holds, for what God is most blamed for in religious circles is His good conscience, His indifference to the quality of His work, and His refusal to mitigate its anomalies. We must have a *future* at any price. Belief in the Last Judgment has created the psychological conditions of a belief in the meaning of history. Better still: all philosophies of history are merely a by-product of the idea of the Last Judgment. However much we may incline toward some cyclical theory, the inclination is only an abstract adherence on our part; we actually behave as if history were following a linear unfolding, as if the various civilizations which have succeeded each other within it were merely stages occupied, in order to manifest and fulfill itself, by some vast design, whose name varies according to our beliefs or our ideologies.

*

Is there a better proof of the inadequacy of our faith than the fact that there are no longer any false gods for us? It is hard to see how for a believer the god he prays to and another quite different god can be equally legitimate. Faith is exclusion, defiance. It is because Christianity can no longer detest the other religions, it is because it *understands* them, that it is finished: the vitality from which intolerance proceeds is in increasingly short supply. Now, intolerance was once Christianity's raison d'être. To its misfortune, it has ceased to be monstrous. Like polytheism in its decline, it is stricken, it is paralyzed by an excessive breadth of views. Its God has no more prestige for us than Jupiter had for the discomfited pagans.

What does the chatter around the "death of God" come down to if not to Christianity's death certificate? We dare not attack religion straight on; we assail the Boss, reproaching Him for being insipid, timid, temperate. No one any longer fears or respects a God who has squandered His capital of cruelty. We are marked by all those centuries when to believe in Him was to fear Him, when our terrors imagined Him at once compassionate and unscrupulous. Whom would He intimidate now, when the believers themselves feel Him by-passed, now that we can no longer connect Him with the present, still less with the future? And just as paganism was to give way before Christianity, so this last God will have to yield to some new belief. Stripped of aggression, He no longer constitutes an obstacle to the outburst of other gods; they need only arrive—and perhaps they will arrive. Doubtless they will not have the countenance nor even the mask of the gods, but they will be no less fearful for that.

For a man to whom freedom and vertigo are equivalent, a faith, wherever it comes from, even if it were antireligious, is a salutary shackle, a desired, a dreamed-of chain whose function will be to constrain curiosity and fever, to suspend the anguish of the indefinite. When this faith triumphs and establishes itself, what immediately results from it is a reduction of the number of problems which we must raise, as well as an almost tragic diminution of choices. The burden of choice is taken from us; options are made for us. The refined pagans who let themselves be tempted by the new religion expected precisely that choices would be made for them, that they would be told where to go, that they no longer need hesitate on the threshold of so many temples nor tack between so many gods. It is by a lassitude, a refusal of the mind's peregrinations, that it comes to an end, this religious effervescence without a credo which characterizes every Alexandrian epoch. We denounce the coexistence of truths because we are no longer satisfied with the *dearth* each one affords. We aspire to the All, but to a limited, a circumscribed, a *sure* All, so great is our fear of declining from the universal into the uncertain, from the uncertain into the precarious and the amorphous. This downfall which paganism knew in its time Christianity is in the process of discovering now. It is failing, it is eager to fail; which makes it endurable to the unbelievers, increasingly well-disposed in its behalf. Paganism, even vanquished, was still detested; the Christians were fanatics who could not forget, whereas in our time everyone has forgiven Christianity. As early as the eighteenth century, the arguments against it were exhausted. Like a venom which has lost its virtues, it can no longer save or damn anyone. But it has toppled too many gods for it to escape, in all justice, the fate it has reserved for them. Their hour of revenge has come round; their joy must be great to see their worst enemy as low as themselves, since it acknowledges them all, without exception. In the time of its triumph, Christianity demolished temples and desecrated consciences wherever it chose to appear. A new god, were he to be crucified a thousand times, knows no pity, crushes everything in his path, strives to occupy the maximum of space. Thus he makes us pay dear for not having recognized him sooner. So long as he was obscure, he could have a certain attraction; we did not yet discern in him the stigmata of victory.

A religion is never "nobler" than when it comes to the point of taking itself for a superstition and witnessing its own eclipse with detachment. Christianity has been formed and has flourished in the hatred of all that was not itself. This hatred sustained it throughout its career; its career finished, its hatred is finished too. Christ will not harrow Hell again: He has been put back in the tomb, and this time he will stay there. It is not likely he will never come forth again: there is no longer anyone to deliver on the surface or in the depths of the earth. When we think of the excesses which accompanied his advent, we cannot help thinking, too, of that exclamation of Rutilius Namatianus, the last pagan poet: "Would to the gods Judea had never been conquered!"

Since it is granted that the gods are true without distinction, why stop halfway, why not preach them all? That would be, on the Church's part, a supreme accomplishment: she would perish bowing before her victims. There are signs to indicate she is not unaware of the temptation. Thus, after the example of the ancient temples, the Church would make it a point of honor to collect the divinities, the derelicts, from everywhere. But, once again, the *true* god must efface himself in order for all the others to rise again.

PALEONTOLOGY

AN UNFORESEEN SHOWER, one autumn day, drove me into the Museum of Natural History for a while. I was to remain there, as a matter of fact, for an hour, two hours, perhaps three. It has been months since this accidental visit, and yet I am not about to forget those empty sockets that stare at you more insistently than eyes, that rummage sale of skulls, that automatic sneer on every level of zoology.

Nowhere is one better served with respect to the past. Here the possible seems inconceivable or cracked. One gets the impression that the flesh was eclipsed upon its advent, that in fact it never existed at all, that it could not have been fastened to bones so stately, so imbued with themselves. The flesh appears as an imposture, a fraud, a disguise which masks nothing. Was this all it was? And if it is worth no more, how does it manage to inspire me with repulsion or with terror? I have always felt a predilection for those who were obsessed by its nullity, those who made a great case for its insignificance: Baudelaire, Swift, Buddha . . . . The flesh, so obvious, is yet an anomaly. The more we consider it, the more aghast we turn away, and, by dint of such weighing, we tend toward the mineral—we grow *petrified*. In order to endure the sight or the idea, we require much more than courage: we require cynicism. We are deceived as to its nature if we call it, with one Church Father, "nocturnal." That would be paying it too much honor. The flesh is neither strange nor shadowy, but *perishable* to the point of indecency, to the point of madness. It is not only the seat of disease, it is itself a disease, incurable nothingness, a fiction which has degenerated into a calamity. The vision I have of it is the vision of a gravedigger infected with metaphysics. Doubtless I am wrong to keep thinking about it; one cannot *live* and lay much stress on it: A colossus would perish in the attempt. I feel it as it is not permitted to feel it; it takes advantage of the fact, it obliges me to confer upon it a disproportionate status and monopolizes me to such an extent that my mind is no more than viscera. Next to the solidity, the *seriousness*, of the skeleton, it seems absurdly provisional and frivolous. It flatters, it gratifies the addict of precariousness I am. That is why I am so comfortable in this museum where everything encourages the euphoria of a universe swept clean of the flesh, the jubilation of an after-life.

At the entrance, man *standing*. All the other animals slumped over, borne down, sagging, even the giraffe, despite its neck, even the iguanodon, grotesque in its effort to pull itself upright. Closer to us, that orangutan, that gorilla, that chimpanzee—easy to see that they have struggled in vain to be erect. Their efforts having failed, they stay where they are, unhappy, arrested halfway, thwarted in their pursuit of verticality. Hunchbacks, in short. We should be like them still, no doubt about it, without the luck we had to take one decisive step forward. Ever since, we labor tooth and nail to eliminate every trace of our low extraction; whence that provocative expression so peculiar to man. Beside him, his posture, and the airs he assumes, even the dinosaurs seem timid. Since his real reverses are only beginning, he will have time to settle down. Everything suggests that, returning to his initial phase, he will rejoin this chimpanzee, this gorilla, this orangutan, that he will resemble them once again, and that it will be increasingly uncomfortable for him to fidget in his vertical posture. Perhaps, indeed, yielding to fatigue, he will be even more bowed than his former companions. Having reached the threshold of senility, he will "re-ape" himself, for one fails to see what would be better for him to do.

*

Much more than the skeleton, it is the flesh, I mean the carrion flesh, which disturbs and alarms us—and which alleviates us as well. The Buddhist monks gladly frequented charnel houses: where corner desire more surely and emancipate oneself from it? The horrible being a path of liberation, in every period of fervor and inwardness, our remains have enjoyed great favor. In the Middle Ages, a man made a regimen of salvation, he believed *energetically:* the corpse was in fashion. Faith was vigorous then, invincible; it cherished the livid and the fetid; it knew the profits to be derived from corruption and gruesomeness. Today, an edulcorated religion adheres only to "nice" hallucinations, to Evolution and to Progress. It is not such a religion which might afford us the modern equivalent of the danse macabre.

"Let a man who aspires to nirvana act so that nothing is dear to him," we read in a Buddhist text. It is enough to consider these specters, to meditate on the fate of the flesh which adhered to them, in order to understand the urgency of detachment. There is no *ascesis* in the double rumination on the flesh and on the skeleton, on the dreadful decrepitude of the one and the futile permanence of the other. It is a good exercise to sever ourselves now and then from our face, from our skin, to lay aside this deceptive sheathe, then to discard—if only for a moment—that layer of grease which keeps us from discerning what is *fundamental* in ourselves. Once the exercise is over, we are freer and more alone, almost invulnerable.

In order to vanquish attachments and the disadvantages which derive from them, we should have to contemplate the ultimate nudity of a human being, force our eyes to pierce his entrails and all the rest, wallow in the horror of his secretions, in his physiology of an imminent corpse. This vision would not be morbid but methodical, a controlled obsession, particularly salutary in ordeals. The skeleton incites us to serenity; the cadaver, to renunciation. In the sermon on futility which both of them preach to us, happiness is identified with the destruction of our bonds. To have scanted no detail of such a teaching and even so to come to terms with simulacra!

Blessed was that age when solitaries could plumb their depths without seeming obsessed, deranged. Their imbalance was not assigned a negative coefficient, as is the case for us. They would sacrifice ten, twenty years, a whole life, for a foreboding, for a flash of the absolute. The word "depth" has a meaning only in connection with epochs when the monk was considered as the noblest human exemplar. No one will gainsay the fact that he is in the process of disappearing. For centuries, he has done no more than survive himself. To whom would he address himself, in a universe which calls him a "parasite"? In Tibet, the last country where monks still mattered, they have been ruled out. Yet it was a rare consolation to think that thousands and thousands of hermits could be meditating there, *today*, on the themes of the *prajñāparamita*. Even if it had only odious aspects, monasticism would still be worth more than any other ideal. Now more than ever, we should build monasteries . . . for those who believe in everything and for those who believe in nothing. Where to escape? There no longer exists a single place where we can professionally execrate this world.

*

In order to conceive, and to steep ourselves in, unreality, we must have it constantly present to our minds. The day we feel it, *see* it, everything becomes unreal, except that unreality which alone makes existence tolerable.

One sign of enlightenment is to have the obsession of the

aggregate, the ever-increasing feeling of being just the place where certain elements come together, welded for the moment. Conceived as a substantial and irreducible datum, the "self" dumbfounds more than its reassures: How to admit that anything that seemed to hold so fast should let go, should stop? How to be parted from what subsists "by itself," from what *is?* We can discard an illusion, no matter how inveterate; but what to do when we are faced with the consistent, with the durable? If there is only what exists, if being spreads everywhere, how do we break away from it without falling to pieces? Let us postulate a universal fallacy out of precaution or therapeutic concern. The fear there is nothing is followed by the fear there is something. We are far more comfortable bidding farewell to nonbeing than to being. Not that this world doesn't exist, but its reality is no such thing. Everything seems to exist and nothing exists.

Every concerted pursuit, even that of nirvana, if we are not free to abandon it, is a shackle as much as any other. The knowledge we convert into an idol is corrupted into an unknowing, as the Vedic wisdom already preached: "They are in the depths of darkness, those who give themselves up to ignorance; those who delight in knowledge are in a darkness deeper still." To think without being any the wiser, or rather not to think at all but to remain *there* and to devour the silence—that is where perspicacity should lead. No pleasure is comparable to that of *knowing* we don't think. It will be objected, Isn't knowing we don't think still thinking? No doubt, but the wretchedness of thought is surmounted for the time that, instead of leaping from idea to idea, we remain deliberately within just one, one which rejects all the rest and which dissolves itself as soon as it takes for its content its own absence. This interference with the normal mechanism of the mind is fruitful only if we can renew it at will. It must cure us of the subjection to knowledge, of the superstition of system. The deliverance which seduces, which beclouds us is not deliverance. We must act so that nothing is ours, beginning with desire, that generator of dread. When everything makes us tremble, the one recourse is to realize that if fear—being a sensation, *the* sensation par excellence—is real, the world which causes it is reduced to a transitory assemblage of unreal elements. In short, our fear is intense in proportion as we give credence to the self and to the world, and that our fear must inevitably diminish when we discover the imposture of the former and of the latter. Only our triumph over things is real, only our realization of unreality, which our acumen constructs every day, every hour. To be delivered is to rejoice in this unreality, to seek it out each moment.

*

Seen from outside, each being is an accident, a lie (except in love, but love is located outside of knowledge, outside the truth). Perhaps we should regard ourselves from outside, somewhat as we regard other people, and try to have nothing further in common with ourselves: If, toward myself, I were to behave as a stranger, I should see myself die with utter unconcern; my death would be "mine" no more than my life. One and the other, insofar as they belong to me and I assume them, represent ordeals beyond my powers. When, on the contrary, I convince myself that they lack intrinsic existence and that they are of no concern to me—what a relief! Why then, knowing that in the last resort everything is unreal, still be carried away for such trifles? I am carried away, granted, but I am not involved, which is to say that I take no *real* interest. This disinterest I cultivate I achieve only when I trade in my old self for a new one, the self of a disabused vision which triumphs here, amid these ghosts, where everything enfeebles me, where the one I was seems to me so remote, so incomprehensible. The evidence on which I used to turn my back now is discernible in all its clarity. The advantage I derive from this is that I no longer feel any obligation with regard to my flesh, to any flesh. A far better context in which to savor the eighteen varieties of void set forth in the Mahayanist texts, so scrupulous in cataloguing the several types of deficiency! For here, instantly, I am in an acute state of unreality.

*

It is scarcely credible to what degree fear adheres to the flesh; it is glued to it, inseparable, almost indistinct from it. These skeletons—happy skeletons!—feel no such thing. Fear is the one fraternal link which joins us to the animals, though they know it only in its natural—its healthy—form, so to speak. They know nothing of that other fear, the one which arises without motive, which we can reduce, depending on our whim, either to a metaphysical process or to a lunatic chemistry and which, daily, at an unpredictable moment, attacks us, overwhelms us. In order to hold it in check, we would require the cooperation of all the erstwhile gods. It reveals itself at the nadir of our daily failure, at the very moment when we would be quite ready to disappear if a mere nothing did not keep us from it; this nothing is the secret of our verticality. To remain erect, standing, implies a dignity, a discipline that has been laboriously inculcated in us and that still saves us at the last minute, in that spasm when we grasp what may be abnormal in the career of the flesh, threatened, boycotted by the sum of elements which define it. The flesh has *betrayed* matter; the discomfort it feels, it endures, is its punishment. In a general way, the animate appears quite guilty with regard to the inert; life is a state of guilt, a state all the more serious in that no one is really conscious of it. But a crime coextensive with the individual, which weighs upon him without his knowledge, which is the price he must pay for his promotion to a separate existence, for the infraction committed against the undivided creation. This crime is no less real for being unconscious and is crucial to the prostration of every creature.

As I circulate among the carcasses, I try to conceive of the burden of fear they must have borne, and when I stop in front of the three apes I cannot fail to attribute the evolutionary hitch they have suffered to an analogous burden which, weighing upon them, has given them that obsequious and flustered expression. And even these reptiles—isn't it under a like load that they have had to grovel so shamefully and to concoct their venom in the dust of the earth, if only to be revenged for their ignominy? Whatever is alive, the most repellent animal or insect, shudders with fear—does nothing but. Whatever is alive, by the simple fact of living, deserves commiseration. And I think of all those I have known, all those who are no more, long since sprawling in their coffins, forever exempt from flesh—and from fear. And I feel relieved of the weight of their death.

Anxiety is consciousness of fear, a fear to the second degree, a fear reflecting upon itself. It consists of the impossibility of communing with the all, of assimilating ourselves with it, of losing ourselves in it. It breaks the current which passes from the world to us, from us to the world, and favors our reflections only to frustrate their growth, ceaselessly disintoxicating the mind. Now there is no speculation of any scope which does not proceed from rapture, from a loss of control, from a faculty to lose and hence to renew the self. Inspiration in reverse, anxiety calls us to heel at the slightest impulse, the slightest divagation. This surveillance is deadly to thought, suddenly paralyzed, trapped in a calamitous circle, doomed never to escape itself except by fits and starts, by stealth. Hence it is true that if our apprehensions make us seek deliverance, yet it is they which keep us from achieving it. Though he dreads the future to the point of making it the sole object of his preoccupations, the anxious man is a prisoner of the past; he is, in fact, the only man who really has a past. His tribulations, of which he is the slave, move him forward only to yank him back. He comes thereby to regret the raw, anonymous fear from which everything starts, the fear that is beginning, origin, principle of everything alive. Terrible as it is, such fear is nonetheless endurable, since whatever lives resigns itself to it. It lacerates and ravages the living—it does not annihilate them. Such is not the case with this refined fear, this "recent" fear posterior to the appearance of the self, in which the diffuse, omnipresent danger is never materialized, a reflexive fear which, for lack of other nourishment, devours itself.

*

If I have not returned to the museum, I have been there in spirit almost every day, thereby deriving considerable advantage: what could be more settling than to brood over this ultimate simplification of beings? A moment comes when the imagination clears and you see yourself as you will be: a sermon—no, a *seizure* of modesty. On the proper use of the skeleton . . . . We should help ourselves to it in difficult moments, especially since we have it right *under our hand.*

I have no need of Holbein nor of Baldung Grien; with respect to the macabre, I rely on my own resources. If I see the necessity for it, or if I am overcome by a craving, there is no one I cannot strip of his carnal envelope. Why envy or fear those bones which bear such and such a name, that skull which has no love for me? Why, too, love someone or love myself, why suffer in any case, when I know the image I must invoke in order to alleviate these miseries? The sharpened consciousness of what lies in wait for the flesh ought to destroy both love and hate. Actually it manages only to attenuate and, in rare moments, to subdue them. Otherwise it would be only too easy: represent death and be happy . . . , and the macabre, gratifying our most secret desires, would be *all profit.*

I suspect that I would never have returned—in flesh or in spirit—so often to those premises if, evidently, they hadn't flattered my incapacity for illusion. Here, where man is nothing, you realize how unsuited the doctrines of deliverance are to understand him, to interpret his past and to decipher his future. This is because deliverance has a content only for each of us, individually, and not for the mob, which is unable to grasp the relation between the idea of emptiness and the sensation of freedom. It is hard to see how humanity might be saved *en bloc*; engulfed in the false, committed to an inferior truth, it will always confuse substance with semblance. Granting, against all appearances, that it is following an ascending path, humanity cannot acquire, at its zenith, the level of insight of even the most obtuse Hindu *sanyāsi*. In everyday existence, it is impossible to say if this world is real or unreal. What we can do, what we do do, is to keep shifting from one thesis to the other, all too happy to evade a choice which would settle none of our immediate difficulties.

Awakening is independent of intellectual capacities: a genius can be a dunce, spiritually speaking. Moreover, knowledge as such gets one no further. An illiterate can possess "the eye of understanding" and thereby find himself above and beyond any scholar. To discern that what you are is not you, that what you have is not yours, to be no longer the accomplice of anything, even of your own life—that is to see clearly, that is to get down to the zero root of everything. The wider you open yourself to vacuity, the more deeply you steep yourself in it, the further you remove yourself from the fatality of being—yourself, of being man, of being alive. If everything is null and void, this triple fatality will be so too. Thereby, the magic of the tragic is exorcised. Is the failing hero worth as little as the hero who finally triumphs? Nothing more glamorous than a splendid ending, if this world is real; if it is not, it is pure foolishness to go into ecstasies over any denouement whatever. To deign to have a "destiny," to be blinded or only tempted by "the extraordinary," proves that we remain opaque to any higher truth, that we are far from possessing "the eye" in question. To situate someone is to determine his degree of awakening, the progress he has made in the perception of the false and the illusory in others, in himself. No communion is conceivable with the man who deceives himself as to what he is. As the interval separating us from our actions widens, we see the subjects of dialogue and the number of our kind diminish. Such solitude does not engender bitterness, for it does not derive from our talents, but from our renunciations. Yet it must be added that it does not in the least exclude the danger of spiritual pride, which certainly exists as long as we nurse the sacrifices we have consented to and the illusions we have rejected. How vanquish ourselves unbeknownst, when detachment demands an insistent sounding of consciousness? Thus, what makes it possible threatens it at the same time. In the order of internal values, any superiority which does not become impersonal turns to perdition. If only one could wrest oneself from the world without realizing the fact! One should be able to forget that detachment is a virtue: otherwise, instead of delivering, it envenoms. To attribute to God our successes of any sort, to believe that nothing emanates from ourselves, that everything is given— that, according to Ignatius Loyola, is the one effective means of struggling with pride. The recommendation is valid for the thunderbolt states in which the intervention of grace seems de rigueur, but not for detachment, an undermining labor, long and painful, of which the *self* is the victim: how fail to pride yourself on that?

Our spiritual level may be raised, yet we do not thereby change qualitatively; we remain prisoners of our limits: the impossibility of uprooting spiritual pride is one consequence of it—the most unfortunate one. "No creature," Saint Thomas observes, "can attain a higher degree of nature without ceasing to exist." Yet if man interests us, it is precisely for having sought to surmount his nature. He has not managed to do so, and his inordinate efforts were not to fail in adulterating, in *denaturing* him. This is why we do not question ourselves in his regard without torment, without passion. No doubt it is also more decent to commiserate with him than with oneself (as Pascal so well understood). In the long run, this passion becomes so tiring that we think of nothing but means of escaping it. Neither the fatality of being oneself nor that of being alive can be compared with that of being man; once that fatality spurs me on, I reconstruct—in order to escape it—my promenade among those bones which, these days, have so often been helpful to me; I recognize them, I cling to them: confirming me in my belief in vacuity, they grant me a glimpse of the day when I shall no longer have to endure the obsession of the human, of all shackles the most terrible. From that we must free ourselves at all costs, if we would be free at all; but to be really free, one more step must be taken: to be free of liberty itself, to reduce it to the level of a prejudice or a pretext in order not to have to idolize it any longer . . . . Only then will we begin to learn how to act without desire. For this the meditation on the horrible prepares us: to circle around the flesh and its decrepitude is to be initiated into the art of dissociating desire and act—an operation fatal to enter-prising minds, indispensable to contemplative ones. So long as we desire, we live in subjection, we are given over to the world; once we cease to desire, we accumulate the privileges of an object and of a god: we no longer depend on anyone. That desire cannot be extirpated is all too true; yet what peace, merely to imagine being exempt from it! A peace so unwonted that a perverse pleasure creeps into it: would not so suspect a sensation come down to nature's revenge upon the man who has made himself guilty of aspiring to a state so unnatural?

Outside of nirvana *in life*—a rare exploit, a virtually inac-cessible extremity—the suppression of desire is a chimera; we do not suppress desire, we suspend it, and this suspension, very strangely, is accompanied by a sense of power, by a new, an unknown, certainty. The vogue of monasticism in past centuries is doubtless explained by this dilation succeeding the ebb of appetites. It takes strength to struggle against desire; this strength increases when desire withdraws; desire halted, fear halts as well. For anxiety, on its part, to conclude any such truce, we must go further; we must confront a much more rarefied space, we must approach an abstract joy, an exaltation granted alike to being and to the absence of being.

It is said in the Katha Upanishad apropos of Atman that it is "joyous and without joy." That is a state to which we accede as well by the affirmation as by the negation of a supreme principle, as much by the detour of Vedanta as by that of Mahayana. Different as they may be, the two paths meet in the final experience, in the glide outside appearances. What is essential is less to know in whose name one seeks liberation than how far one can advance on the path to it. Whether one is dissolved into the absolute or into the void, in either case it is a neutral joy one achieves: a joy without any determination, as denuded as the anxiety of which it seeks to be the remedy, and of which it is merely the outcome, the positive conclusion. Between them, the symmetry is patent; they may each be said to be "constructed" on the same model; they dispense with any external stimulant, they are self-sufficient, they correspond and communicate in depth. For just as concrete joy is only a vanquished fear, neutral joy is only a transfigured anxiety. And it is from their affinities, from their permeability, that the possibility derives of mounting from one to the other, and the danger of falling back, of a regression to an earlier state supposedly transcended. Which suggests to what degree all spiritual progress is threatened at its base. For the unfulfilled seeker after deliverance, for the beginner in nirvana, nothing is easier, nothing more frequent than to retreat toward his old terrors. But when, at long intervals, he manages to hold fast, he makes his own the exhortation of the Dhammapada, "Shine for yourself, as your own light," and, during the time he adopts and follows it, he understands, from within, those who conform to it always.

ENCOUNTERS WITH SUICIDE

YOU KILL YOURSELF only if, in some respects, you have always been outside of it all. What is involved is an original dispossession of which you cannot be conscious. A man *called* to kill himself belongs only accidentally to this world; he is in fact answerable to no world at all.

You are not predisposed, you are predestined to suicide; you are committed to it before any disappointment, before any experience: happiness impels you to it as much as misery does, even more, for happiness—amorphous, improbable— requires an exhausting effort of adaptation whereas misery offers security and the rigor of a rite.

*

There are nights when the future cancels out, when only one of all its moments subsists, the one we shall choose in order to exist no longer.

*

The further I go, the more I see my chances dwindle of dragging myself from one day to the next. To tell the truth, it has always been like this: I have not lived in the possible, but in the inconceivable. My memory accumulates prostrate horizons.

*

There exists in us a temptation, rather than a will, to die. For it were granted to us to *will* death, who would not take advantage of it at the first vexation? Another obstacle also intervenes: the idea of killing himself seems incredibly new to the man who is possessed by it; he therefore imagines himself performing an action *without precedent*; this illusion fills and flatters him, and causes him to waste precious time.

*

Suicide is a sudden accomplishment, a lightninglike deliverance: it is nirvana *by violence.*

*

So simple a fact as looking at a knife and realizing that it depends only on yourself to make a certain use of it gives you a sensation of sovereignty which can turn to megalomania.

*

When the idea of putting an end to it all takes hold of us, a space opens out before us, a vast possibility outside of time and of eternity itself, a dizzying issue, a hope of dying *beyond* death.

To kill yourself is, thereby, to compete with death, to prove that you can do better than death, to put one over on death and—no negligible success—to redeem yourself in your own eyes. You are reassured, you thus convince yourself that you are not the worst, that you deserve some respect. You tell yourself: up to now, incapable of taking any initiative, I had no self-esteem; now everything is changed: destroying myself, I thereby destroy all the reasons I had to despise myself, I regain confidence, I am *someone* forever. . . .

*

Since it is my mission to suffer, I do not understand why I try to imagine my fate otherwise, still less why I rage against *sensations.* For that is what all suffering is, at the start and at the end in any case. In the middle, of course, it is something more: a universe.

*

This passion in the middle of the night, this insistence on a final explanation with yourself, with the elements. . . . Suddenly your blood seethes, you tremble, you get up, go out, remind yourself there is no longer any reason to beat around the bush, to procrastinate: this time it will be for good. No sooner are you outside than you feel, almost imperceptibly, a kind of relief. You walk on imbued with the gesture you are about to make, with the mission you have assigned yourself. A touch of exaltation replaces the passion when you tell yourself that at last you have come to the end, that the future has come down to a few minutes, to an hour at the most, and that you have decreed, on your own authority, the suspension of time's total.

Then comes the reassuring impression which the absence of others inspires: everyone else is asleep. How to abandon a world in which you can still be alone? This night, which was to be the last, is the one you cannot part with, you do not conceive that it might be eliminated. And you would like to defend it against the day which undermines and soon submerges it.

*

If we could change our nature, become anyone else, we should belong from the start to the elect. Since metamorphosis is not to be realized, we cling to predestination, a magic word if ever there was one. Merely uttering it gives us the sensation of having passed beyond the stage of questions and perplexities, of having found at last the key to every deadlock.

*

When you feel the longing to be done with it all, whether weak or overwhelming, you are led to reflect upon it, to explain it, to explain it to yourself. You are especially likely to do this, moreover, when the longing is weak, for when it is too intense it invades the mind and leaves it neither space nor time to consider or to escape it.

*

To wait for death is to suffer it, to expect death is to reduce it to the rank of a process, to resign yourself to a denouement whose date, décor, and manner you know nothing about. You are far from the absolute action. Nothing in common between the obsession with suicide and the sentiment of death— I mean that profound, constant feeling of an end in itself, of a fatality to perish as such, inseparable from a cosmic background and independent of that drama of the self at the center of any form of autodestruction. Death is not necessarily experienced as deliverance; suicide always is: it is a *summum*, the paroxysm of salvation.

We should, out of decency, choose for ourselves the moment to disappear. It is debasing to die the way one does; it is intolerable to be exposed to an end over which we have no control, an end which lies in wait for us, overthrows us, casts us into the unnameable. Perhaps the moment will come when a natural death will be altogether discredited, when we shall enrich the catechisms with a new formula: "Grant us, Lord, the favor and the force to end it all, the grace to eliminate ourselves in time."

The age-old conspiracy against suicide is responsible for the congestion and the sclerosis of societies. We must learn to destroy ourselves *at the right moment*, to run joyously toward our ghost. So long as we do not determine to do so, we deserve our humiliations. When a man has exhausted his raison d'être, it is odious to persist . . . . But this, indeed, is the indignity of natural death which we discover wherever we happen to look.

"Meeting, after several years, someone we used to know as

a child, the first glance almost always suggests that some great disaster must have befallen him" (Leopardi). To last is to lessen: existence is loss of being. Since no one dies when he should, we ought to call to order anyone who survives himself, encourage and if need be assist him to abbreviate his days. After a given moment, to persevere is to assent to decay. But be sure of your decline. Might you not be mistaken about the symptoms? Does not consciousness of decay imply a superiority to decay itself? And, in that case, have you decayed yet? How, once again, know if you have begun the descent, how determine that moment? Mistakes are certainly possible, but they are of no consequence, since to all intents and purposes you never die on time. You drift, and it is only when you flow with the current that you confess you are flotsam. And then it is too late to sink of your own free will.

*

It is comforting to think that you are going to kill yourself. No subject is more restful: as soon as you approach it, you breathe. To meditate upon suicide is almost as liberating as the act itself.

The more marginal I am to the moments, the more the prospect of severing myself from them forever reincorporates me with existence, puts me on a proper footing with the living, confers a kind of standing. This prospect, which I cannot do without, has rescued me from all my dejections, has allowed me, above all, to survive those periods when I had no grievance against anyone, when I was content. Without its help, without the hope it affords, paradise would seem to me the worst of torments. How many times have I murmured to myself that without the notion of suicide one would kill oneself on the spot! The mind it engrosses coddles it, idolizes it, expects miracles from it. Like a drowning man who clings to the idea of shipwreck.

*

There are as many reasons to eliminate yourself as there are reasons to continue, with the difference, however, that the latter have more seniority, more solidity. They weigh more heavily than the former because they are identified with our origins, whereas the former, the fruit of experience, being necessarily more recent, are both more urgent and more uncertain.

*

The same man who says, "I don't have the courage to kill myself," will the next moment call cowardly an exploit before which the bravest would cringe. You kill yourself, we are forever being told, out of weakness, in order not to have to face suffering or shame. Only no one sees that it is precisely the weak who, far from trying to escape suffering or shame, accommodate themselves to such feelings—and that it requires vigor in order to win free of them decisively. In truth, it is easier to kill yourself than to vanquish a prejudice as old as man, or at least as his religions, so sadly impermeable to the supreme gesture. So long as the Church was rampant, only the madman enjoyed the favors of the regime, he alone had the right to put an end to his days: His corpse was neither profaned nor hanged. Between ancient stoicism and modern "free thought," between, say, Seneca and Hume, suicide suffered—aside from the Catharist interlude—a long eclipse, a dark age in fact, for all those who, wanting to die, dared not infringe the ban on putting oneself to death.

*

The infirmities which we have observed and analyzed lose their gravity and their strength; once examined, we endure them better. With the exception of sadness. The degree of "performance" which is involved in depression is inapplicable to sadness; intransigent, intractable, sadness knows nothing of imagination, whimsy. With sadness, there is no escape clause, no flirtation. And no matter how much we talk about it, comment upon it, sadness neither diminishes nor increases. It *is*.

*

The man who has never contemplated killing himself will bring himself to do so much more promptly than the man who thinks about it all the time. Every crucial act being easier to perform by thoughtlessness than by scrutiny, the mind virgin of suicide, once it feels impelled in that direction, will have no defense against this sudden impulsion; it will be blinded and shaken by the revelation of a final solution which it had not previously considered. Whereas the man who is *suicide prone* can always procrastinate a gesture which he has endlessly weighed and weighed again, which he knows through and through, and to which he will bring himself without passion, if he ever brings himself to it at all.

*

The horrors that glut the universe constitute an integral part of its substance; without them, the universe would *physically* cease to exist. To draw the ultimate consequences of this phenomenon is not to commit a "beautiful" suicide. The only kind which deserves this epithet is the kind which springs up out of nowhere, without apparent motive, for no reason: pure suicide. It is this suicide—a defiance to all capital letters—which humiliates, which crushes God, Providence, and even Fate.

*

A man does not kill himself, as is commonly supposed, in a fit of madness but rather in a fit of unendurable lucidity, in a paroxysm which may, if so desired, be identified with madness; for an excessive persipicacity, carried to the limit and of which one longs to be rid at all costs, exceeds the context of reason. The culminating moment of the decision testifies nonetheless to no darkening of the mind: technical idiots virtually never kill themselves, but you can kill yourself from a fear, from a foreboding of idiocy. The act itself is then inseparable from the last spasm of the mind which *recovers* itself, which musters all its powers, all its faculties, before cancelling itself out. On the threshold of the final defeat, it proves to itself that it is not completely lost. And it loses itself in full and instantaneous possession of all its powers.

*

We have unlearned the art of killing ourselves *cold*. The ancients were the last to excel in it. The suicide we conceive of is ardent, feverish, an inspired state; as for detachment, it is as convulsionaries that we dream of it. Those sages who antedated the Cross knew how to break with this world or resign themselves to it, without drama, without lyricism. Their style has been lost, as well as the basis of their imperturbability: a usurping Providence came to dislodge *Fatum* from every cranny. And we rush to recover it, craving support there, when no other can guide or beguile us.

*

There is nothing more profound nor more incomprehensible than desire. Which is why we feel we are alive only when we despair of destroying it.

*

Whether we do away with ourselves or not, everything remains unchanged. But the decision to do away with ourselves seems to each of us the most important that has ever been taken. It should not be so. And yet it is so, and nothing can prevail against this aberration or this mystery.

*

Having always coincided only with the interval which separates me from beings, from things, with the void which opens in the center of each of my sensations, how could I help being amazed at seeing myself subscribe to anything whatever, endorse my remarks, adhere to my vacillations, even my convictions? So much naïveté torments me, and reassures me.

*

You must be greedy for the absolute in order to envisage suicide. But you can also envisage it by doubting—by doubting everything. It's quite natural: the more you seek the absolute, the deeper, out of resentment at your incapacity to find it, you sink into doubt, which is the opposite of a quest, the negative conclusion of a great crusade, a grand passion. The absolute is a pursuit; doubt, a retreat. This retreat, a pursuit in reverse, collides, when it cannot stop, with extremities inaccessible to rational procedure. At first it was only a method; now it is an intoxication, like everything which tends beyond the self. To advance or to retrogress toward limits, to plumb the depths of anything, is to encounter, necessarily, the temptation of self-destruction.

*

On that minor Mediterranean island, long before sunrise, I was making my way along the path leading to the steepest cliff and thinking the thoughts of a vacationing concierge: if I had that villa I'd paint it ocher, I'd have a different fence put up, etc. Despite *my* idea, I was clinging to every straw: I stared at the century plants, I dawdled, I shrouded in digressions the urgency of my intention. A dog began barking, then made friends and followed me. You cannot imagine, if you haven't experienced it, the solace of an animal coming to keep you company when the gods have turned their backs.

*

Facing a landscape annihilated by the light, to remain serene supposes a temper I do not have. The sun is my purveyor of black thoughts; and summer the season when I have always reconsidered my relations with this world and with myself, to the greatest prejudice of both.

*

When you have understood that nothing *is*, that things do not even deserve the status of appearances, you no longer need to be saved, you are saved, and miserable forever.

*

I try—without success—to stop finding reasons for vanity in anything. When I happen to manage it nonetheless, I feel that I no longer belong to the mortal gang. I am above everything then, above the gods themselves. Perhaps that is what death is: a sensation of great, of extreme superiority.

*

Jean Paul calls the most important night of his life the one when he discovered there was no difference between dying the next day or in thirty years. A revelation as significant as it is futile; if we occasionally manage to grasp its cogency, we resist on the other hand drawing its consequences, in immediacy the difference in question seeming to each of us somehow irreducible, even absolute: to exist is to prove that we have not understood to what point it is all one and the same thing to die now or no matter when.

Though I may know that I am nothing, it still remains for me to convince myself of it authentically. Something, inside, rejects this truth of which I am so certain. This rejection indicates that I partially escape myself; and what in me escapes my jurisdiction and my control makes me forever uncertain of being able to dispose of myself altogether. It is in this way that by everlastingly repeating the pros and cons of the one gesture that matters, we reach the point of having a bad conscience about still being *alive*.

*

The obsession with suicide is characteristic of the man who

can neither live nor die, and whose attention never swerves from this double impossibility.

*

So long as I act, I believe that what I do involves a "meaning," otherwise I could not do it. Once I cease acting and transform myself from an agent to a judge, I no longer recover the meaning in question. Next to the self who is what I do, there is another one (the self's self) who is superior to what I do: for this self, what I do and even what I am implies neither meaning nor reality: it is as if remote events were involved, events forever past, whose apparent reasons we decipher without perceiving their intrinsic necessity. They might quite simply not have been, so external to us are they . . . . This same perspective, applied to the whole of an existence, leads straight to the rumination upon the extravagance of being born at all.

In the same way, if you were to ask, apropos of any action, what would be its result in a year, in ten years, in a hundred or a thousand, it would be impossible to complete or even to commence it. Every action supposes a limited vision, except the action of killing yourself, for this action proceeds from an enormous vision, one so vast that it makes all other actions vain and unattainable. Juxtaposed to it, everything is futility and mockery. It alone proposes a way out, I mean an abyss— a *liberating* abyss.

*

To reckon on anything at all, here or elsewhere, is to afford proofs that we are still burdened with chains. The reprobate aspires to paradise; this aspiration disparages, compromises him. To be free is to rid yourself forever of the notion of reward, it is to expect nothing of men or gods, it is to renounce not only this world and all worlds but salvation itself—it is to destroy even the notion of it, that chain among chains.

*

What matters is to combat the instinct of self-preservation—pure stubbornness and nothing else; what matters is to combat that instinct by denouncing its ravages. There is all the more likelihood we shall succeed when we rehabilitate suicide, when we emphasize its excellence, when we make it joyous and accessible to all. Anything but a negative act, suicide, on the contrary, redeems, transfigures all previous actions.

By the most inexplicable of misunderstandings, existence has been declared sacred; not only is it no such thing, but it is worth something only insofar as we undertake to keep it from being so. It is at best an accident—an accident which little by little each of us converts into a fatality. When we know what to expect in its regard, we blush to attach ourselves to it, and we attach ourselves to it nonetheless by a long and gradual process which obliges even the most enlightened among us to take it seriously. We should, by a converse process, reduce existence to its original state, to its primal insignificance. An effort neighboring on the miraculous would be required: the man who made it would cease being a slave; master of his days, he would halt their succession when he chose; his existence would be *at his discretion*; this is because it would have rejoined its point of departure, its true status: that of an accident, precisely.

*

To live entirely without a goal! I have glimpsed this state, and have often attained it, without managing to remain there: I am too weak for such happiness.

*

If this world emanated from an honorable god, to kill yourself would be an audacity, a nameless provocation. But since there is every reason to believe that this world is the work of a sub-god, it is hard to see why we should go to the trouble. To spare *Whom*?

Profiting greatly from the recession of faith, suicide will be increasingly easy and, thereby, less mysterious since it will have used up its prestige as an anathema. Once piquant and praiseworthy, it is now becoming what can be done—it is gaining ground, and if it has stopped being astonishing, its future, on the other hand, seems assured. Inside the religious universe, it appeared as an insanity and a betrayal, the transgression par excellence. How can a man believe and annihilate himself? Let us fall back on the hypothesis of the sub-god, which has the advantage of permitting extreme gestures, the radical victory over a flawed world.

We can imagine this creator, conscious at last of his miscalculation, acknowledging his guilt: he desists from it, withdraws, and, by a last twinge of elegance, does away with himself. Thus he vanishes with his opus, without man's having had a hand in it. Such would be the improved version of the Last Judgment.

*

Suicides prefigure the far-off fates of humanity. They are harbingers, and as such we must respect them. Their hour will come; they shall be celebrated, given public homage, and we shall say that they alone, *in the past*, had envisaged all, had divined all. We shall also say that they had made the first move, that they had sacrificed themselves in order to point the way, that they were, in their fashion, martyrs: had they not killed themselves in epochs when no one was obliged to do so, and when a natural death was all the rage? Before the rest, they knew that *impossibility* pure and simple would one day be the lot of all; instead of being a curse, a privilege.

Precursors, so they will be called; and so they were, even as those who, conscious of the sovereignty of evil, have incriminated the creation: the Manicheans early in the Christian era, and to a singular degree their belated disciples, the Cathari. The admirable thing is that this incrimination was, among the latter, more frequent among the people than among the lettered. To be convinced, we need merely consult Bernard Gui's *Practica Inquisitionis* or any other report of the period on the ideas and actions of the "heretics." Here we shall find— a comforting detail—some tanner's wife or, say, a woodcutter's at grips with Lucifer or denouncing our first ancestors as guilty of "the most Satanic of all actions." These sectarians, or rather these visionaries, so curiously disabused in the midst of their fervor, endowed with the gift of scenting the diabolic snares behind all our important actions, could let themselves starve to death if need be; and this exploit, not at all uncommon among them, marked the pinnacle of their doctrine. To put oneself in *endura*, to fast to death, was a practice following upon initiation; its mission was to preserve the "consoled" from the peril of apostasy or from all kinds of temptations.

The disgust with the *useful* aspect of sexuality, the horror of procreation, constitutes part of the interrogation of the creation: what is the good of multiplying monsters? Had it triumphed, and had it remained faithful to itself, Catharism would have led to a collective suicide. Such a success was hardly possible: however advanced they were, men's minds were not sufficiently ripe. Even today, they are still far from being so, and we must wait a long time before humanity puts itself in *endura*. Supposing that it ever does so.

*

In the Council of 1211 against the Bogomils, those among them were anathematized who held that "woman conceives in her womb by the cooperation of Satan, that Satan abides there upon conception without withdrawing hence until the birth of the child."

I dare not suppose that the Devil can be concerned with us to the point of keeping us company for so many months; but I cannot doubt that we have been conceived under his eyes and that he actually attended our beloved begetters.

*

This sensation of being jammed for eternity, of having served one's term before being born, of falling too far to find anyone to commiserate with, this certitude that by killing yourself you kill no one—this is the temptation of the *bad* suicide, of the one which rises up not from the melancholy according to God but according to the Devil, to keep the Apostle's distinction. It is also comfortlessness in its highest degree and which seems so irremediable that it would remain intact, unbroached, were another universe to be started up.

What is that "brief and vehement" prayer which the desert fathers recommend against lapses and terrors?

*

Why don't I kill myself? If I knew *exactly* what keeps me from doing so, I should have no more questions to ask myself since I should have answered them all.

*

To keep from tormenting yourself, you must sink into a profound disinterestedness, you must stop being intrigued by the mundane or by the beyond, falling instead into the indifference of the dead. How can you look at a living man without imagining him a corpse, how can you contemplate a corpse without putting yourself in its place? *Being* is unthinkable, *being* unmans . . . .

*

Someone altogether good will never bring himself to take his own life. This exploit requires a vein—or vestiges—of cruelty. A man who kills himself might, under certain conditions, have killed others: Suicide and murder belong to the same family. But suicide is more refined, for cruelty to yourself is rarer, more complex; not to mention that it includes the intoxication of feeling pulverized by your own consciousness.

A man whose instincts are compromised by goodness neither

intervenes in his fate nor tries to forge another; he yields to the one he has, resigns himself, and continues, a stranger to exasperation, arrogance, and malice which, together, invite and facilitate self-destruction. The notion of hastening his end never occurs to his . . . modesty: Indeed, it takes a morbid modesty to submit to dying in any way except by your own hand.

*

How to conceive that a prayer might be anything except a monologue, that an ecstasy might have any value beyond itself, that our salvation or our perdition might matter to a god?

And yet this is what you would have to be able to admit, if only for one second each day.

*

The future, that precipice, so fells me that I should like to see even the notion of it disappear. Actually it is that notion, much more than the slither into the abyss which it conceals, that has me shivering in my shoes and keeps me from enjoying the present. My reason staggers before everything that happens, before everything that is to happen. It is not what awaits me, it is waiting in itself, imminence as such, which erodes and appalls me. To regain a semblance of peace I must cling to a time without tomorrow, to a decapitated time.

*

No matter how often I rehash the formula of triple renunciation—"I reject this world, I reject the world of the ancestors, I reject the world of the gods"—when I measure the space separating me from sackcloth and the desert I remind myself of a fairground *sanyāsi*.

*

Isn't regret a sign of precocious aging? If so, I am senile from birth.

*

You haven't seen to the bottom of a thing if you haven't considered it in the light of prostration.

*

Only those moments count when the desire to remain by yourself is so powerful that you'd prefer to blow your brains out than to exchange a word with someone.

*

The hard thing, for a man who has renounced halfway, is to do the rest. Existence doubtless burdens him, but he has not exhausted his surprise at existence. Which accounts for his vacillations, and the remorse at having stopped in between, with no opportunity to fulfill an intention conceived long ago. One of renunciation's failures.

*

It is our sufferings which give some weight to our thoughts and keep them from turning into pirouettes; it is also our sufferings which make us proclaim that there is no such thing as reality—that even our sufferings have none. Hence they suggest a defense strategy: we triumph over them by declaring them unreal, by linking them to the general deception. If they were endurable, what need would there be of diminishing them, of exposing them? Since we have no other way out except to identify them with either nightmare or whim, it is easiest to opt for the latter.

All things considered, it would be best if there were nothing. If something *existed*, we should live in the apprehension of being able to apprehend it. Since there is nothing, all moments are perfect and null, and it is indifferent whether or not we enjoy them.

*

The only way of dissuading someone from suicide is to urge him to do it. He will never forgive you for your gesture, he will abandon his scheme or postpone its execution, he will regard you as an enemy, as a traitor. You thought you were rushing to his aid, rescuing him, and he sees in your eagerness no more than hostility and contempt. The strangest thing of all is that he was seeking your approval, pleading for your complicity. What did he actually expect? Haven't you deceived yourself as to the nature of his confusion? What a mistake on his part to turn to you! At this stage of his solitude, what should have struck him is the impossibility of coming to an understanding with anyone except God.

*

We are all deranged, we take for real what is not so. A living man as such is mad and blind both: Incapable of discerning the illusory aspect of things, he sees solidity, fullness, everywhere. If by some miracle he happens to see the truth, he lays himself open to vacuity and flourishes there. Richer than the reality it replaces, vacuity takes the place of everything *without everything*; it is basis and absence, abyssal variant of being. But to our misery, we regard it as a deficiency; whence our fears and our failures. What is vacuity for us after all? At most a diaphanous impasse, an impalpable inferno.

*

Diligent in extenuating, in reducing his appetites to nothingness, he has managed only to derange them, to strip them of whatever was healthy, was stimulating about them: a thwarted, undermined beast of prey, regretting his former instincts. His claws being blunted but not the desire to use them, all his violence is turned to desolation (for desolation is nothing but wounded aggression, an aggression humiliated, impotent to make the most of itself).

He has begun by sabotaging his passions; then his beliefs. The process was inexorable. This revelation which presided over his days—to adhere to anything is to participate in infan-

tilism or madness—might be legitimate enough; he may subscribe to it still; it is nonetheless excruciating, intolerable. It
permits him to endure but not to exist, it belongs to those
certitudes a man never gets over.

Contentious and quarrelsome by nature, he no longer con-
tends, no longer picks fights; at least no longer with others.
The blows once intended for them he now belabors himself
with—he himself is the target. Himself? What self? There is
no one left to strike: no more victim, no more subject, nothing but a succession of actions without agent, nothing but an
anonymous parade of sensations . . . .

Is he released—or merely wrecked? Saved—or merely a spook?

*

"What shall it profit a man, if he shall gain the whole
world, and lose his own soul?" To gain the world, to lose your
soul! I've done better than that: I've lost both.

*

Whatever I attempt, it will never be anything but the
demonstration of a downfall, patent or camouflaged. For a
long time, I worked out the theory of the outsider, the man
apart from it all. This man I have now become, I incarnate
him. My doubts have materialized, my negations are made
flesh. I live what once I imagined myself living: At last I have
found myself a disciple.

THE UNDELIVERED

THE MORE WE CONSIDER the Buddha's last exhortation, "Death is inherent in all created things; labor ceaselessly for your salvation," the more we are troubled by the impossibility of *feeling* ourselves as an aggregate, a transitory if not fortuitous convergence of elements. We readily conceive ourselves as such in the abstract; in the immediate, we physically gainsay it, as if we were faced with some unassimilable evidence. So long as we have not triumphed over this organic repugnance, we shall continue to suffer that illusion-based scourge which is the craving to exist.

That we unmask things, that we stigmatize them with the name of appearances counts for nothing, for we admit thereby that they harbor being. We cling to anything, if only we don't have to tear ourselves away from that fascination accountable for our actions and even our nature, from that primal dazzle which keeps us from discerning the nonreality in everything.

I am a "being" by metaphor; if I were one in fact, I should remain so forever, and death, stripped of meaning, would have no hold on me. "Labor ceaselessly for your salvation"— that is, don't forget that you are a fugitive assemblage, a composite whose ingredients are only waiting to come apart. Salvation, indeed, has a meaning only if we are provisional to the point of mockery; if there were the slightest principle of duration in us, we should have been forever saved or lost: no more quest, no more horizon. If deliverance matters at all, our unreality is a real godsend.

*

We should deprive being of all its attributes, make it no longer the support, the site, of all our attachments, the eternal reassuring impasse, a prejudice—the most deeply rooted of all, the one we are most accustomed to. We are accomplices of being, or of what seems so to us, for there is no being, there is only the ersatz of being. If there were a true one, we should still have to release ourselves from it, extirpate it, since everything which *is* turns to subjection and shackles. Let us ascribe to others the status of shades; we shall separate ourselves from them all the more easily. If we are mad enough to believe they exist, we expose ourselves to nameless miscalculations. Let us have the prudence to acknowledge that everything that happens to us, every event, like every bond, is inessential, and that if there is a knowledge, what it must show us is the advantage of maneuvering among ghosts.

Thought, too, is a prejudice, a shackle. It liberates only at the beginning, when it permits us to break certain moorings; afterwards, all it is capable of is to absorb our energy and to paralyze our impulses toward liberation. That it can help us in no way is sufficiently proved by the happiness we feel when we suspend it. Like desire, to which it is related, thought feeds on its own substance; it likes to manifest, to multiply itself. At best, it can tend toward truth, but what defines thought is *bother:* We think by a liking for thought, as we desire by a liking for desire. In either case, a fever amid fictions, an over-exertion within nescience. The man who knows has recovered from all the fables engendered by desire and by thought; he leaves the current, no longer consents to the deception. To think is to participate in the inexhaustible illusion which begets and devours itself, greedy to perpetuate and destroy itself; to think is to compete with delirium. In so much fever, the only sensible thing is the pause when we breathe, the moments of suspension when we get the better of our hard breathing: the experience of the void—which is identified with the totality of such pauses, of such intervals in delirium—implies the momentary suppression of desire, for it is desire which plunges us into nescience, which sets us straying, which drives us to project being all around us.

The void allows us to erode the idea of being; but it is not drawn into this erosion itself; it survives an attack which would be self-destructive for any other idea. It is true that the void is not an idea but what helps us rid ourselves of any idea. Each idea represents one more mooring; we must free the mind of them, as we must free ourselves of all beliefs, those obstacles to withdrawal. We shall succeed only by raising ourselves above the operations of thought: as long as thought functions, as long as thought is rife, it keeps us from discerning the depths of the void, perceptible only when the fevers of the mind and of desire diminish.

All our beliefs being intrinsically superficial and governing only appearances, it follows that all are on the same level, at the same degree of unreality. We are constituted to live with them, we are constrained to do so: They form the elements of our ordinary, everyday malediction. This is why, when we happen to expose them and sweep them away, we enter into the unheard-of, into an expansion next to which everything seems pale, episodic, even that very malediction. Our limits retreat, if we have any left. The void—myself without me—is the liquidation of the adventure of the "I"—it is being without any trace of being, a blessed engulfment, an incomparable disaster.

(The danger is to convert the void into a substitute for being, and thereby to thwart its essential function, which is to impede the mechanism of attachment. But if the void itself becomes the object of attachment, would it not have been wiser to abide by being and the cortege of illusions which follows it? In order to throw off our fetters, we must learn to adhere to nothing any longer, if not to the *nothing* of freedom.)

*

Ideally, we should lose—without suffering from the loss— our liking for beings and for things. Every day we should honor someone, creature or object, by renouncing them. Thereby we should arrive, inventorying appearances and dismissing them one after the other, in perpetual withdrawal, the very secret of joy. Everything that we appropriate, our knowledge even more than our material acquisitions, merely feeds our anxiety; on the other hand, what calm, what radiance when that frenzied pursuit of possessions, even spiritual ones, abates! It is already a serious matter to say "me," more serious still to say "mine," for that supposes an additional collapse, a reinforcement of our allegiance to the world. It is a consolation, the notion that we possess nothing, that we are nothing; the supreme consolation resides in the victory over this notion as well.

So closely does anxiety adhere to being, that it must tear itself away if it would overcome itself. If it aspires to rest in God, it will succeed in doing so only insofar as He is superior to being or at least insofar as He contains a zone where being is reduced or rarefied: it is here that, no longer having anything to contend with, anxiety is freed and approaches those confines where God, liquidating His last vestiges of being, lets Himself be tempted by the void.

*

The sage, as the East has always known, refuses to make plans, never *projects*. Hence you would be a kind of sage . . . . To tell the truth, you make plans, but it revolts you to carry them out. The more you brood over one, the more you feel, abandoning it, a well-being which can reach the point of ecstasy.

Everyone lives in and on the project, consequence of nescience: a metaphysical confusion on the scale of the species. For the awakened, becoming, and a fortiori every action which is inserted within it, is no more than a lure, a deception begetting disgust or dread.

What matters is not to produce but to understand. And to understand signifies to discern the degree of awakening to which a being has achieved, his capacity to perceive the sum of unreality which enters into each phenomenon.

*

Let us abide by the concrete and the void, let us proscribe whatever is located between the two: "culture," "civilization," "progress." Let us brood over the best formula ever devised here on earth: manual labor in a monastery . . . . There is no truth, except in physical expenditure and in contemplation; the rest is accidental, useless, unhealthy. Health consists in exercise and in vacuity, in muscles and meditation; in no case in thought. To meditate is to be absorbed into an idea and to be lost there, whereas to think is to leap from one idea to the next, to delight in quantity, to accumulate trifles, to pursue concept after concept, goal after goal. To meditate and to think are two divergent, even incompatible activities.

To abide by the void—is this not also a form of pursuit? No doubt, but it is to pursue the absence of pursuit, to aim at a goal which sets aside all the others from the start. We live in anxiety because no goal can satisfy us, because over all our desires, and a fortiori over being as such, floats a fatality which necessarily affects those accidents which are individuals. Nothing of what becomes *actual* escapes forfeiture. The void —a leap outside this fatality—is, like every product of quietism, antitragic in essence. Thanks to the void we might learn to recover ourselves by climbing back toward our origins, toward our eternal virtuality. Does it not put an end to all our desires? And they—what are they, taken together, next to a single moment when we pursue none, when we feel none! Happiness is not in desire but in the absence of desire, more precisely in our enthusiasm for that absence—in which we would like to wallow, to sink, to vanish, to *exclaim* . . . .

*

When the void itself seems too heavy for us or too impure, we hurl ourselves toward a nakedness beyond any conceivable form of space, while the last moment of time rejoins the first one and dissolves into it.

*

Let us scour consciousness of everything it includes, of every universe it drags in its wake, let us purge ourselves along with perception, confine ourselves to white, let us forget all the colors except the one which denies them. What peace, once we annul diversity, once we escape the calvary of nuance and are engulfed in the uniform! Consciousness as pure form, then the very absence of consciousness.

To elude the intolerable, let us seek out a counterirritant, a means of avoidance, a region where no sensation condescends to take a name, nor any appetite to be made flesh—let us recover that initial repose and abolish, with the past, odious memory and consciousness above all, our age-old enemy whose mission it is to impoverish us, to erode us. Unconsciousness, on the contrary, is nutritive, it fortifies, it makes us participate in our beginnings, in our primal integrity, and plunges us back into beneficent chaos, the chaos before the trauma of individuation.

*

Nothing matters: a great discovery, if ever there was one, from which no one has been able to gain any advantage. To this discovery, supposedly a depressing one, only the void, of which it is the motto, can give a stirring resonance; only the void takes its place, takes the place of everything, fulfills all the irreparable into the possible. That there is no self we know, but our knowledge is encumbered with reservations. Luckily the void is there, and when the self is withdrawn the void takes its place, takes the place of everything, fulfills all our expectations, affords us the certitude of our nonreality. The void—the abyss *without vertigo*.

Instinctively, we incline to the self; everything in us lays claim to it: It satisfies our demands for continuity, for solidity, it confers upon us, against all evidence, a timeless dimension: Nothing more normal than to cling to it, even when we put it in question, divulge its impostures: The self is any living man's *reflex* . . . . All the same it seems inconceivable for us once we consider the self coldly: it crumbles, it vanishes, it is nothing more than the symbol of a fiction.

Our first movement bears us toward the intoxication of identity, toward the dream of indistinction, toward Atman, which answers our deepest, most secret summons. But as soon as we gain a little perspective, coming to our senses, we abandon the supposed basis of our being, turning toward the fundamental destructability, knowledge and experience of which, a disciplined obsession, lead to nirvana, to *plenitude* within the void.

*

It is because it gives us the illusion of permanence, it is because it promises what it cannot provide, that the idea of the absolute is suspect, not to say pernicious. Assailed at the roots of our being, utterly unfit to last, perishable to our very essence, it is not consolation we require but cure. The absolute neither resolves our perplexities nor suppresses our ills: It is merely a makeshift and a palliative. A doctrine which extols it is true insofar as it confines itself to analysis, insofar as it exposes appearances; it inspires doubts as soon as it confronts them with an ultimate reality. Once we leave the realm of the illusory and struggle to substitute the indestructible for it, we skid into falsehood. If we lie less with the void, it is because we do not seek it out for itself, for the truth it is supposed to contain, but for its therapeutic virtues; we make it into a remedy, we imagine it will correct the mind's oldest deviation, which consists in supposing that something exists. . . .

A compromised animal, man has passed the stage of being content with a "hope"; what he expects is not just another artifice, but deliverance. Who will bring it to him? On this point, the only one that matters, Christianity has shown itself less helpful than Buddhism, and Western speculation less effective than Oriental. Why bother with abstractors deaf to our cries or with redeemers busy rubbing salt into our wounds? And what is still to be hoped for from this part of the world which regards contemplation as abulia, awakening as torment?

We need some saving shock. It is incredible that a Saint Thomas should have seen in stupor an "obstacle to philosophic meditation," whereas it is precisely when we are "stupefied" that we begin to understand, that is, to perceive the inanity of all "truths." Stupor benumbs us only to awaken us the more readily: it opens to us, it releases us to the essential. A complete metaphysical experience is nothing but an uninterrupted stupor—a triumphal stupor.

*

It is a sign of indigence to be unable to open ourselves to the purifying void, the void that appeases. We are so low, and so entangled in our philosophies that we have been able to conceive only nothingness, that sordid version of the void. We have projected all our uncertainties, all our miseries and terrors there, for what is nothingness, finally, but an abstract complement of hell, a performance of reprobates, the maximum effort toward the lucidity available to beings unsuited for deliverance? Too tainted by our impurities for it to let us make the leap toward a virgin concept such as the void is for us (the void, which has not inherited from, "taken after" hell, which is not contaminated by it), nothingness, in truth, represents only a sterile extremity, only a disconcerting, vaguely funereal way out, quite close to those attempts at renunciation which turn sour because too much regret is mixed in with them.

The void is nothingness stripped of its negative qualifications, nothingness transfigured. If we should manage to develop a taste for it, our relations with the world are transformed; something in us changes, though we keep our old defects. But we are no longer from *here* in the same way as before. This is why it is salutary to resort to the void in our crises of rage: our worst impulses are blunted upon that contact. Without the void, who knows, we might now be in prison or in some padded cell. The lessons in abdication it teaches also invite us to a subtler behavior with regard to our denigrators, our enemies. Should they be killed, or spared? Which does more harm, which gnaws deepest: vengeance, or victory over vengeance? How decide? In our uncertainty, let us choose the torture of not taking revenge.

Such is the limit-concession we can make if we are not saints.

*

Only the man oppressed by the universality of torment is ripe for deliverance. To try to free yourself without the awareness of this torment is either an impossibility or a vice. There is no gratuitous deliverance; we must be liberated from something, in this case from the omnipresence of the intolerable—which we suffer as much in the hypothesis of being as of non-being, since things and the appearances of things make us suffer equally. But the hypothesis of vacuity offers an advantage after all: it casts a clearer light over the excess of the torment, over the proportions it assumes and the inanity of the cause which provokes it. We always torture ourselves too much, whether this world is real or unreal. The majority, it is true, are unaware of how much they are suffering. It is the privilege of consciousness to waken to the excruciating, to perceive the throbbing illusion to which human beings are in thrall.

It is with deliverance as it is with Christian salvation: some theologian, in his scandalous naïveté, believes in redemption even while denying original sin; but if sin is not consubstantial with humanity, what meaning can we attribute to the advent of the redeemer? What has he come to redeem? Anything but accidental, our corruption is permanent, it is congenital. The same with iniquity: abusively charged with "mystery," iniquity is an evidence, it is even what is most visible here on earth, where to put things back in order would require a savior for each generation, or rather for each individual.

*

Once we cease to desire, we become the citizen of all worlds and of none. It is by desire that we are from *here*; desire vanquished, we are no longer from anywhere and have nothing further to envy a saint nor a specter.

It may happen that there is happiness in desire, but beatitude appears only where every bond is broken. Beatitude is not compatible with this world. It is for beatitude that the hermit cuts all his moorings, for beatitude that he destroys himself.

*

Cow's urine was the only medicine monks were authorized to use in the first Buddhist communities. One cannot imagine a more judicious restriction. If we pursue peace, we shall reach it only by rejecting whatever is a factor of disturbance, whatever man has grafted onto simplicity, onto his original health. Nothing exposes our failure better than the spectacle of a pharmacy: all the remedies desirable for each of our ills, but none for our essential ill, for the disease of which no human invention can cure us.

*

If believing ourselves unique is the result of an illusion, it is, let us admit, an illusion so total, so imperious that we are entitled to wonder if we can still call it one. How desist from what we shall never recover, from that pathetic and unheard-of nothing which bears our name? The illusion in question, source of all the pangs we must suffer, is so deeply anchored in each of us, that we can vanquish it only by means of a sudden whirlwind which, sweeping away the ego, leaves us alone, without anyone, without ourselves. . . .

Unfortunately, we cannot exterminate our desires; we can only weaken them, compromise them. We are up against the self, infected with the venom of the "I." It is when we escape it, when we imagine we escape it, that we have some right to use the high words employed by the true (and the false) mysticism. As for a fundamental conversion, there is no such thing: we convert *with our nature.* Even the Buddha after illumination was only Siddhartha Gautama *with knowledge in addition.*

Everything we believe we have smothered rises to the surface again after a certain time: defects, vices, obsessions. The most patent imperfections we have "corrected" return disguised but as awkward as before. The pains we have taken to rid ourselves of them will not, however, have been altogether in vain. A desire, long supplanted, reappears; but we *know* it has come back; it no longer gnaws us in secret nor takes us unawares; it dominates us, subjugates us, we are still its slaves, true, but not consenting slaves. Every *conscious* sensation is a sensation we have unsuccessfully opposed. We are not the more pained for that, since its victory will have driven it from our deepest life.

*

In each encounter we have chosen what is easiest: God or His substitutes, *persons* in any case, in order to have someone to gossip or argue with. We have replaced contemplation with tension, thereby creating tiresomely emotional relations between divinity and ourselves. Only men who seek but are unwilling to *find* could have become virtuosi of the inner drama. The great modern discovery is spiritual malaise, the quartering between substance and vacuity, more precisely between the simulacre of each. Whence the cult of singularity, in every realm. In literature, a rare mistake is worth more than any tried, acknowledged truth. The unwonted, on the contrary, has no value on the spiritual level, where all that matters about an experience is its depth.

According to the Bhagavadgita, a man is lost to this world and to the other who is "given over to doubt," that same doubt which Buddhism, for its part, cites among the five obstacles to salvation. This is because doubt is not depth or a search for depth but stagnation, the vertigo of stagnation. With doubt, it is impossible to advance, to arrive; doubt is corrosion and nothing but. When we suppose ourselves farthest from it, we relapse into it, and everything begins all over again. It must *explode* for us to be able to take the path of emancipation. Without this outburst which must pulverize even the most legitimate reasons for doubting, we perpetuate ourselves in malaise, we cultivate it, we avoid the great solutions, we corrode ourselves and delight in our corrosion.

*

The passion to withdraw, to leave no trace, is inaccessible to anyone attached to his name and to his work, and even more inaccessible to anyone who dreams of a name or a work—

the trifler in short. Such a man, if he persists toward salvation, will achieve it, at best, only by *bogging down* in nirvana.

*

We do not conceive of a *bitter* mystic. Knowledge according to the world, clairvoyant aridity, excessive lucidity without an inner dimension, bitterness is the appanage of the man who, having cheated in his relations with the absolute and with himself, no longer knows what to hold onto nor whom to turn to. Bitterness is after all more frequent than we suppose, it is normal, everyday, the common lot. Joy, on the other hand, fruit of an exceptional moment, seems to rise up out of a disequilibrium, a derangement in the depths of our being, so contradictory is it to the appearances where we live. And if it were to come from elsewhere, from further than ourselves? Joy is expansion, and every expansion participates in another world, whereas bitterness is constriction, even if infinity looms in the background. But it is an infinity which crushes instead of liberating.

No, it is inconceivable that joy should be deranged, still less that it should come from nowhere; joy is so complete, so enveloping, so marvelously unendurable that we cannot confront it without some supreme reference. In any case it is joy and joy alone which allows the notion that we can forge gods *out of our need for gratitude.*

*

It is not difficult to imagine the language a contemporary man would use if he were obliged to declare his opinion about the only religion which has contributed a radical formula for salvation:

"The search for deliverance is justified only if we believe in transmigration, in the indefinite vagabondage of the self, and if we aspire to put an end to it. But for those of us who do not believe in this, what is there to put an end to? To this unique and infinitesimal duration? It is obviously too brief to deserve the exertion of withdrawing from it. For the Buddhist, the prospect of other existences is a nightmare; for us, the nightmare is the cessation of this one—of this nightmare. As for nightmares, better give us another, we should be tempted to cry out, in order that our disgraces not end too soon, in order that they have time to follow us through several lives . . . .

"Deliverance corresponds to a necessity only for the man who feels threatened by an additional existence, who dreads the task of dying and dying all over again. For us, condemned not to be reincarnated, what is the use of struggling to liberate ourselves from . . . nothing? to free ourselves from a terror whose end is in sight? And what is the use of pursuing a supreme unreality, when everything here on earth is already unreal? Why bother ridding ourselves of something so little justified, so *unfounded*? . . .

"An increase in illusion and in torment, that is what each of us aspires to, each of those who have no opportunity to believe in the endless circle of births and deaths. We sigh for the curse of being reborn. The Buddha has really taken too much trouble to what end? A *definitive* death: what the rest of us are sure to obtain without meditations or mortifications, without any effort whatever . . . ."

It is more or less in this manner that our fallen man would express himself, if he consented to expose his real thoughts. And who would dare cast the first stone? Who hasn't spoken this way to himself? We have sunk so deep into our own history that we want it to be perpetuated without respite. But whether we live once or a thousand times, whether we own one hour or all of them, the problem is the same: an insect and a god would not differ in their way of considering the fact of existing as such, which is so terrifying (as only a miracle can be) that when we linger over it, we conceive the desire to disappear forever, in order not to have to consider it again in other existences. It is on this phenomenon that the Buddha has insisted, and it is doubtful that he would have modified his conclusions if he had ceased believing in the mechanism of transmigration.

*

To find that everything lacks reality and not to put an end to it all, this inconsistency is not an inconsistency at all: taken to extremes, the perception of the void coincides with the perception of the whole, with the entrance into the All. At last we begin to see, we grope no longer, we are reassured, we are confirmed. If a chance of salvation exists outside of faith, it is in the faculty of *enriching ourselves* upon contact with unreality that we must seek it.

Even if the experience of the void were only a deception, it would still deserve to be tried. What it proposes, what it attempts, is to reduce to nothing both life and death, and this with the sole intention of making them endurable to us. If it occasionally succeeds, what more can we desire? Without it, no cure for the infirmity of being, nor any hope of reinstating, even for a few moments, the prenatal joy, the light of pure previousness.

STRANGLED THOUGHTS

I

ENDLESS BROODING OVER a question undermines you as much as a dull pain.

*

In what ancient author did I read that melancholy was caused by "slowing" of the blood? Just what it is: *stagnant* blood.

*

You are done for—a living dead man—not when you stop loving but stop hating. Hatred preserves: in it, in its chemistry, resides the "mystery" of life. Not for nothing is hatred still the best tonic ever discovered, for which any organism, however feeble, has a tolerance.

*

Think of God and not religion, of ecstasy and not mysticism. The difference between the theoretician of faith and the believer is as great as between the psychiatrist and the psychotic.

*

It is in the nature of a rich mind not to shrink from foolishness, that scarecrow of the finicky—whence the latter's sterility.

*

To make more plans than an explorer or a crook, yet to be infected at the will's very root.

*

Refinement is the sign of deficient vitality, in art, in love, and in everything.

*

What is a "contemporary"? Someone you'd like to kill, without quite knowing how.

*

Each moment's tug of war between nostalgia for the deluge and intoxication with routine.

*

To have the vice of scruple—to be an automaton of remorse.

*

Terrifying happiness. Veins in which thousands of planets distend.

*

The most difficult thing in the world is to put yourself in tune with being, to catch its *pitch*.

*

Sickness gives flavor to want, it intensifies, it *picks up* poverty.

*

The mind advances only if it has the patience to go in circles, in other words, to *deepen*.

*

First duty, on getting up in the morning: to blush for yourself.

*

Fear will have been the inexhaustible nourishment of his life. He was swollen, stuffed, obese with fear.

*

The lot of the man who has rebelled too much is to have no energy left except for disappointment.

*

No assertion is more false than Origen's, according to which each soul has the body it deserves.

*

In every prophet coexist a craving for the future and an aversion for happiness.

*

To want fame is to prefer dying scorned than forgotten.

*

To remember suddenly that you have a *skull*—and not to lose your mind over it!

*

Suffering makes you live time in detail, moment after moment. Which is to say that it exists for you: over the others, the ones who don't suffer, time flows; so that they don't live in time, in fact they never have.

*

The only man who knows what it feels like to be accursed is the man who knows he would have that feeling in the middle of paradise.

*

All our thoughts are a function of our ailments. If we understand certain things, the credit for it goes to the gaps in our health—and to them alone.

*

If he didn't believe in his "star," he couldn't perform the merest action without an effort: to drink a glass of water would seem a gigantic, even a deranged undertaking.

*

What they ask you for is actions, proofs, works, and all you can produce are transformed tears.

*

An ambitious man resigns himself to obscurity only after having exhausted all the reserves of bitterness he possessed.

*

I dream of a language whose words, like fists, would fracture jaws.

*

To enjoy only hymns, blasphemy, epilepsy. . . .

*

To conceive a thought—just one, but one that would tear the universe to pieces.

*

Only insofar as we do not know ourselves is it possible for us to realize and to produce ourselves. Fruitful is the man who is mistaken as to the motives of his actions, who resists weighing his qualities and defects, who foresees and dreads the impasse into which the exact view of our capacities leads us. The creator who becomes transparent to himself no longer creates: to know oneself is to smother one's endowments and one's demon.

*

There is no means of *proving* it is preferable to be than not to be.

*

"Never let melancholy assail you, for melancholy forbids all good," says Tauler's sermon on the "Right Use of the Day." The wrong use I have made of each of my days!

*

I have repressed all my enthusiasms; but they exist, they constitute my reserves, my unexploited resources, perhaps my future.

*

The mind *staved in* by lucidity.

*

My doubts have not been able to get the better of my automatisms. I continue to make gestures to which it is impossible for me to adhere. To overcome the drama of this *insincerity* would be to renounce, to annul myself.

*

We really believe only as long as we are unaware that we must implore. A religion is alive only before the elaboration of its prayers.

*

Every form of impotence and failure involves a positive character *in the metaphysical order*.

*

Nothing could persuade me that this world is not the fruit of a dark god whose shadow I extend, and that it is incumbent upon me to exhaust the consequences of the curse hanging over him and his creation.

*

Psychoanalysis will be entirely discredited one of these days, no doubt about it. Which will not keep it from having destroyed our last vestiges of naïveté. After psychoanalysis, we can never again be innocent.

*

The very night when I asserted that our dreams had no relation to our innermost life and that they derived from bad literature, I fell asleep only to be the onlooker at the procession of my oldest and most hidden terrors.

*

What is called "strength of mind" is the courage not to imagine our fate *otherwise*.

*

A writer worthy of the name confines himself to his mother tongue and does not go ferreting about in this or that alien idiom. He is limited, and likes to be—out of self-defense. Nothing wrecks a talent more certainly than a mind too wide open.

*

The moralist's primordial duty is to depoeticize his prose; only then, to observe men.

*

"How badly nature has conceived us!" an old woman once said to me. "It is nature herself that is badly conceived," I should have answered, if I had heeded my Manichean reflexes.

*

Irresolution has become virtually a mission for him. Anyone at all made him despair of all his resources. He was incapable of making a decision *in front of* a face.

*

All things considered, it is pleasanter to be surprised by events than to have anticipated them. When we exhaust our powers in the vision of disaster, how are we to confront disaster itself? Cassandra torments herself doubly, before and during the calamity, whereas the optimist is spared the pangs of prescience.

*

According to Plutarch, by the first century of our era men went to Delphi only to ask trivial questions (marriage, investments, etc.). The decadence of the Church imitates that of the oracles.

*

"The naive is a nuance of vulgarity": Fontenelle. There are certain remarks which are the key to a country, because they yield us the secret of its limits.

*

Napoleon, on Saint Helena, liked to leaf through a grammar from time to time . . . . Thereby, at least, he proved he was *French*.

*

Sunday afternoon. Streets filled with a haggard, exhausted, pitiable crowd—rejects from everywhere, vestiges of continents, scum of the earth. One thinks of Rome under the Caesars, overrun by the dregs of the Empire. Every world center is a city dump.

*

The disappearance of animals is a phenomenon of unprecedented gravity. Their executioner has invaded the landscape; there is no room left for anyone or anything but him. The horror of finding a man where you could contemplate a horse!

*

Insomnia's role in history, from Caligula to Hitler. Is the impossibility of sleeping the cause or the consequence of cruelty? The tyrant *lies awake*—that is what defines him.

*

A beggar's remark: "When you pray beside a flower, it grows faster."

*

Anxiety is not difficult, it adapts itself to everything, for there is nothing which fails to please it. At the first excuse, an eminently miscellaneous occurrence, it presses in, fondles, taps a mediocre but certain malaise on which it feeds. Anxiety is content with little enough, anything will serve. Ineffectual trifler, anxiety lacks class: it tries for anguish, and falls short.

*

How does it happen that in life as in literature, rebellion, however pure, has something false about it, whereas resignation, however tainted with listlessness, always gives the impression of authenticity?

*

Squatting on the banks of the Seine, several million soured souls elaborate a nightmare in common which the rest of the world . . . . envies.

*

What is commonly called "being expressive" is being prolix.

*

His sterility was infinite: it partook of ecstasy.

*

The certitude of failing my obligations, of not doing what I was born for, of letting the hours go by without taking advantage of them, even a negative advantage. This last reproach is is not justified though—boredom, my running sore, being precisely that paradoxical advantage.

*

To be naturally combative, aggressive, intolerant—and to be unable to appeal to any dogma!

*

Confronted with this bug the size of a comma running across my desk, my first reaction was charitable: to squash it. Then I decided to abandon the creature to its panic: what was the use of liberating it? Only, I should so much have liked to know *where* it was going!

*

An anxious man constructs his terrors, then installs himself within them: a stay-at-home in a yawning chasm.

*

Impossible to know why an idea seizes upon us and will not let us go. As if it rose up out of the weakest point of our mind or, more exactly, out of the most *threatened* point of our brain.

*

Expert at dissimulating his pride, the sage is someone who does not *deign* to hope.

*

That sudden tension, that sense that something is happening, that the mind's fate is being decided. . . .

*

Madness is perhaps merely an affliction *which no longer develops*.

*

Those moments when it seems impossible for us ever to disappear, when life and death lose all reality, when neither one nor the other can touch us yet . . . .

*

It is a mistake to identify dejection and thought. Were we to do so, anyone who felt depressed would automatically become a thinker. The worst of it is, he does.

*

The experience of inanity, of the void, sufficient unto itself, also involves such philosophic virtues that one fails to see why we should look elsewhere. What does it matter if we discover nothing by this experience if by this experience we understand everything!

*

Living is an impossibility of which I have unceasingly become aware, day after day, for, say, forty years. . . .

*

Memory's one function is to help us *regret*.

*

I can distinctly imagine the moment when there will no longer be a trace of flesh anywhere, and yet I go on as if it made no difference. How define this state in which consciousness does not weaken desire, in which it actually stimulates desire, the way—it is true—the worm *wakens* the fruit?

*

The continuity of reflection is thwarted and even broken each time the brain's physical presence is felt. This is perhaps the reason why the mad think only in *flashes*.

*

Sometimes you feel like shouting to the ci-devant gods: "Oh, exert yourselves a little, just try to re-exist!" Grumble as I will against everything that *is*, I am nonetheless attached to it—judging by these discomforts that are related to the first symptoms of being.

*

The skeptic is the least mysterious of men, and yet, starting from a certain moment, he no longer belongs to this world.

II

A work cannot rise up out of indifference nor even out of serenity, that sifted, fulfilled, victorious indifference. At the height of an ordeal, we are surprised to find so few works that can calm and comfort us. How could they, when they themselves are the product of disturbance and discomfort?

*

Every beginning of an idea corresponds to an imperceptible lesion of the mind.

*

On the mantelpiece, the photograph of a chimpanzee and a statuette of the Buddha. This proximity, more accidental than intentional, makes me wonder over and over *where* my place might be between these two extremes, between man's pre- and transfiguration.

*

Not the excess but the absence of fear is morbid. I think of that friend whom nothing ever frightened, a woman who couldn't even imagine a danger, of any kind. So much freedom, so much safety, was one day to lead her straight to a straight-jacket.

*

In our certainty of not being understood, there is as much pride as shame. Whence the equivocal character of any failure. We are proud of it on the one hand, mortified on the other. How impure any defeat!

*

Incurable—an honorific that should be applied to only one disease, the most terrible of all: desire.

*

It is unjust to call imaginary the diseases which are, on the contrary, only too real, since they proceed from our mind, the only regulator of our equilibrium and of our health.

*

Every neophyte being a spoilsport, once someone gets excited over anything, even my own vagaries, I prepare for a rift—and my revenge.

*

Inclined toward resentment, I often give in to it and brood over it, and stop only when I *recall* that I have envied one sage or another—that I have even thought I resembled him.

*

Those moments when you want to be absolutely alone because you're sure that, face to face with yourself, you will be able to discover rare, unique, unheard-of truths—then disappointment and thereafter bitterness, when you find that once this solitude is achieved at last, nothing comes out, nothing could come. . . .

*

At certain times, instead of the brain, the very exact sensation of usurping nothingness, that steppe which has substituted itself for ideas.

*

To suffer is to *produce* knowledge.

*

Thought is destruction in its essence. More precisely: in its *principle.* You think, you begin to think, in order to break bonds, to dissolve affinities, to compromise the scaffolding of the "real." Only later, when the sapper's work is well under way, does thought recover itself and rebel against its natural movement.

*

Whereas sadness is justified as much by reasoning as by observation, joy rests on nothing, it derives from divagation. Impossible to be joyous by the pure fact of living; we are sad on the other hand as soon as we open our eyes. Perception as such produces melancholy, witness the animals. Only mice seem to be gay without effort.

*

On the spiritual level, all pain is an opportunity; on the spiritual level alone.

*

I can undertake nothing without setting aside what I know. Once I envisage that, once I think of that, even if only for a second, I lose courage, I undo myself.

*

Since things continue to get worse from generation to generation, to predict catastrophes is a normal activity, a duty of the mind. Talleyrand's remark about the Old Regime suits any period, except the one in which you are living, and the one in which you are going to live. The "sweetness" in question is continually diminishing; one day it will have vanished altogether. In history, we are always on the threshold of the worse. . . . That is what makes history interesting, what makes us hate it, and be unable to detach ourselves from it.

*

We may be sure that the twenty-first century, more advanced than ours, will regard Hitler and Stalin as choirboys.

*

Basilides the Gnostic is one of the rare minds to have understood, early in our era, what now constitutes a commonplace, i.e., that humanity, if it wants to be saved, must return within its natural limits by a return to ignorance, true sign of redemption. This commonplace, we hasten to say, is still a clandestine one: each of us murmurs it, but is careful not to declare it aloud. When it becomes a slogan, a considerable step forward will have been taken.

*

In everyday life, men act out of calculation; in their decisive choices, they please themselves, and we understand nothing of either individual or collective dramas if we lose sight of this unexpected behavior. No one should concern himself with history if he fails to realize how rarely the instinct of self-preservation is manifested in it. Everything occurs as if the defense-mechanisms functioned only in the presence of everyday dangers and failed in the face of a major disaster.

*

Consider the face of the man who has succeeded, who has *struggled*, in any realm. You will not find there the slightest trace of pity. He has the stuff out of which enemies are made.

*

For days at a time, the longing to perpetrate an attack against the five continents, without a moment's thought as to the *means*.

*

My energy awakens only *outside of time*, and I feel myself a veritable Hercules as soon as I transplant myself in imagination to a universe where the very conditions of action are suppressed.

*

"The horror and the ecstasy of life"—experienced simultaneously, as though within the same moment, within each instant.

*

The quantity of exhaustion that *rests* in my brain!

*

What I have in common with the Devil is bad humor—I am, like him, crabby by divine decree.

*

The books I read with most interest concern mysticism and dietetics. Might there be some relation between them? Yes, doubtless, insofar as mysticism implies *ascesis*, which is to say a regimen, more precisely a diet.

*

"Eat nothing you have not sown and harvested with your own hand"—this recommendation of Vedic wisdom is so legitimate and so convincing that, in one's rage over being unable to abide by it, one would like to let oneself starve to death.

*

Stretching out, I close my eyes. Suddenly an abyss yawns, like a well that, in search of water, perforates the ground with a dizzying speed. Swept into this frenzy, into this void endlessly begetting itself, I identify myself with the generating principle of the abyss and—unhoped-for happiness—I thereby find an occupation and even a mission.

*

When Pyrrho conversed, if his interlocutor left he continued talking as if nothing had occurred. This power of indifference, this discipline of disdain I dream of with all the impatience of derangement.

*

What a friend expects are accommodations, deceptions, consolations, all things which imply effort, the labor of reflection, self-control. The permanent preoccupation with delicacy which friendship supposes is antinatural. Give me enmity or indifference, so I can breathe a little!

*

By all the emphasis I lay on my miseries, past and future, I have neglected those of the present: which has permitted me to endure them more readily than if I had spent my reserves of attention upon them.

*

Sleep would be good for something if each time we dropped off we tried to see ourselves die; after a few years' training, death would lose all its prestige and would seem no more than a formality or a pinprick.

*

In the career of a mind which has liquidated prejudice after prejudice, there comes a moment when it is quite as easy to become a saint as a swindler in any line.

*

Cruelty—our oldest characteristic—is rarely described as borrowed, simulated, apparent; labels proper, on the other hand, to kindness, which, being recent, acquired, has no deep roots: It is a belated invention, and an intransmissible one. Each of us struggles to reinvent it, and succeeds only by fits and starts in those moments when his nature is eclipsed, when he triumphs over his ancestors and himself.

*

Often I imagine myself climbing up on the roof, getting dizzy, and then, on the point of falling, letting out a scream. "Imagine" is not the word, for I am *obliged* to imagine this. The thought of murder must come in the same way.

*

If you want never to forget someone, to think of him constantly, to attach yourself to him forever, you must not set about loving him, but hating. According to a Hindu belief, certain demons are the fruit of a vow, made in a previous life, to be incarnated in a being dead set against God, in order to be able to meditate upon Him the better and to have Him ceaselessly present to the mind.

*

Death is the aroma of existence. Death alone lends savor to the moments, alone combats their insipidity. We owe death almost everything. This debt of recognition which we now and then consent to pay is what is most comforting here on earth.

*

It is during our insomnias that pain fulfills its mission, that it materializes, blossoms. Then pain is as limitless as the night, which it *imitates*.

*

We should suffer no sort of anxiety so long as we have the notion of bad luck. As soon as we invoke it, we are comforted, we endure anything, we are almost content to suffer injustices and infirmities. Since anything becomes intelligible thereby, we must not be surprised that idiot and illuminated alike resort to it. This is because bad luck is not an explanation, it is *the* explanation, which is reinforced by the inevitable failure of all the others.

*

Once we scrutinize the merest memory, we are ready to burst with rage.

*

What is the source of that monotonous vision of ours, when the ills which have provoked and sustained it are so unaccountably diverse? The fact is that this vision has assimilated them and preserved only their essence, which is common to them all.

*

Chatter: any conversation with someone who has not suffered.

*

Midnight. Tension bordering on epilepsy. Craving to make everything blow up, efforts not to explode in fragments. Imminent chaos. You can be worth nothing by yourself, and be someone by what you feel. But you can also not be worthy of your sensations.

*

In theory, it matters as little to me whether I live as whether

I die; in practice, I am lacerated by every anxiety which opens an abyss between life and death.

*

Animals, birds, insects have resolved everything long since. Why try to do better? Nature loathes originality, nature rejects, execrates *man*.

*

Torment, for some men, is a need, an appetite, and an accomplishment. Everywhere they feel diminished, except in hell.

*

In the blood an inexhaustible drop of vinegar: to what fairy do I owe it?

*

An envious man forgives you nothing, he will envy even your embarrassments, even your shames.

*

The mediocrity of my grief at funerals. Impossible to feel sorry for the deceased; conversely, every birth casts me into consternation. It is incomprehensible, it is insane that people can *show* a baby, that they can exhibit this potential disaster and rejoice over it.

*

You are obsessed by detachment, purity, nirvana, and yet someone in you whispers: "If you had the courage to formulate your most secret wish, you would say: 'I'd like to have invented all the vices.' "

*

There is no point in being a monster if you are not also a theoretician of the "monstrous."

*

You have let what was best in you die. More careful, you would not have betrayed your true vocation, which was that of the tyrant or the hermit.

*

To turn against yourself at every opportunity is to give evidence of a great concern for truth and justice; it is to indict and to strike the real criminal. Unfortunately it is also to intimidate and paralyze him, and thereby to make him unlikely to improve.

*

These rages which strip you of skin and flesh, reducing you to the state of a trembling skeleton!

*

After certain nights, we should change names, since we are also no longer the same man.

*

Who are you? I am an *alien* to the police, to God, to myself.

*

For years, I have gone into ecstasies over the virtues of impassibility, and a day doesn't pass that I don't suffer a fit of violence which, unrepressed, would justify the asylum. These convulsions generally occur without witnesses but, in fact, almost always on account of someone. My rages lack breeding: They are too plebeian, too earthy, to be able to emancipate themselves from a cause.

*

Impossible for me to deal with anything external, objective, impersonal, unless it should be *ills*, i.e., what in others makes me think of myself.

*

The desolation expressed by a gorilla's eyes. A funereal mammal. I am descended from that gaze.

*

Whether we consider the individual or humanity as a whole, we must not identify *to advance* with *to progress,* unless we admit that going toward death is progress.

*

The earth is apparently five billion years old—life, two or three. These figures contain every consolation we could hope for. We should remember them in the moments when we take ourselves seriously, when we *dare* suffer.

*

The more we stammer, the more we struggle to write better. Thus we take revenge for not having been able to be an orator. The stutterer is a born stylist.

*

What is difficult to understand are fruitful, generous natures, always content to be working, to be producing. Their energy seems excessive, and yet one does not quite envy them. They can be anything, because at bottom they are nothing: dynamic puppets, nullities with inexhaustible gifts.

*

What keeps me from going down into the arena is that I see too many minds there I admire but do not esteem, so naive do they seem to me. Why provoke them, why measure myself against them on the same track? My lassitude grants me such a superiority that it seems (to me) quite impossible they should ever catch up.

*

We can think of death every day and yet persevere quite cheerfully in being. This is not the case if we think unceasingly of the *moment* of our death; the man who had only that in view would be committing an outrage against all his other moments.

*

People are astonished that France, a frivolous nation, should have produced a Rancé, founder of the austerest order of all; perhaps they should be even more astonished that Italy, more frivolous still, should have given the world a Leopardi, the most serious of all poets.

*

Germany's drama is not to have had a Montaigne. What luck for France to have *begun* with a skeptic!

*

Disgusted by the nations, I turn to Mongolia, where it must be good to live, where there are more horses than men, where the Yahoo has not yet triumphed.

*

Every fruitful idea turns into a pseudo-idea, degenerates into a belief. Only a sterile idea preserves its status as an idea.

*

I imagined myself more exempt from vanity than others: A recent dream was to disabuse me. I had just died. A coffin of planks was brought. "You could have put a little varnish on it, even so!" I exclaimed before belaboring the undertakers with my fists. An uproar ensued. Then came the awakening, and shame.

*

This fever which leads to no discovery, which bears no idea, but which gives you a feeling of quasidivine power, power which fades once you try to define it—what does it correspond to, and what can it be worth? Perhaps it has no relation to anything, perhaps it goes further than any metaphysical experience.

*

Happiness is to be outside, to walk, to look, to amalgamate

with things. Sitting down, you fall victim to the worst of yourself. Man was not created to be nailed to a chair. But perhaps he doesn't deserve any better.

*

During my insomnia I tell myself, as a kind of consolation, that these hours I am so conscious of I am wresting from nothingness, and that if I were asleep they would never have belonged to me, they would never even have existed.

*

"To lose oneself in God"—this believer's cliché assumes a revelatory value for the nonbeliever, who in it discerns a longed-for and impracticable adventure, despairing as he does of being unable to *stray*, he too, into something or, preferably, someone.

*

Who is superficial? Who is profound? To go very far into frivolity is to cease being frivolous; to reach a limit, even in farce, is to approach extremities of which, in his line, any metaphysician is quite incapable.

*

An elephant would succumb to these fits of depression that is indistinguishable from a cruelty on the point of dissolving and which, dissolving, would sweep away flesh and blood. Every organ is involved: visceral calamity, sensation of gastric surfeit, of impotence to digest this world.

*

Man, that exterminator, has designs on everything that lives, everything that moves: soon we shall be talking about the last louse.

*

In the Trojan War, as many gods on one side as the other. A just and elegant view of which the moderns, too impassioned or too vulgar, are incapable, insisting that the *right* be partisan at any price. Homer, at the start of our civilization, granted himself the luxury of objectivity; at the antipodes, in a belated period like ours, there is no longer room for anything but *attitude*.

*

Alone, even doing nothing, you do not waste your time. You do, almost always, in company. No encounter with yourself can be altogether sterile: Something necessarily emerges, even if only the hope of some day meeting yourself again.

*

So long as you envy another's success, even if it is a god's, you are a vile slave like everyone else.

*

Each being is a broken hymn.

*

According to Tolstoy, we should desire only death, since this desire, unfailingly realized, will not be a deception like all the rest. Yet is it not desire's essence to tend toward anything, except death? To desire is to want not to die. If then we begin wanting death, it is because desire is diverted from its proper function; it is a deviated desire, raised up against the other desires, all committed to disappoint, whereas this one always keeps its promises. To bet on this one is to be sure of winning, no matter what: This desire does not, cannot deceive. But what we expect of a desire is precisely that it deceive us. Whether or not it is realized, that is secondary; the important thing is that it hides the truth from us. If it reveals the truth it fails in its duty, it compromises and abjures itself and consequently must be struck from the list of desires.

*

Attracted though I am by Buddhism, or Catharism, or any

system or dogma, I preserve a core of skepticism which nothing can ever penetrate and to which I always return after each of my enthusiasms. Whether this skepticism is congenital or acquired, it seems to me no less of a certitude, even a liberation, when every other form of salvation blurs or rejects me.

*

Other people do not have the feeling that they are charlatans, and they are; I . . . I am one as much as they but I know it and suffer from that.

*

That I should continue to sabotage my powers—is it not childish to chide myself for that? Yet instead of flattering me, the evidence of my lack of accomplishment discourages me, shatters me. To be intoxicated with lucidity and be no further than this! I drag vestiges of dignity which dishonor me.

*

Only a writer without a public can allow himself the luxury of being sincere. He addresses no one: at most, himself.

*

A full life is, in the best of cases, merely an equilibrium of drawbacks.

*

When you know that every problem is only a false problem, you are dangerously close to salvation.

*

Skepticism is an exercise in defascination.

*

Everything, in the end, comes down to desire or to the absence of desire. The rest is nuance.

*

I have maligned life so much that, wanting for once to do it justice, I find no word that fails to ring false.

III

Sometimes it seems better to realize yourself than to let yourself go, sometimes it seems the contrary. And you are quite right in both cases.

*

Our virtues, far from reinforcing each other, actually envy and exclude each other: When we grow conscious of their warfare, we begin to denounce them one by one, only too pleased not to have to take any futher trouble for any of them.

*

What we want is not freedom but its appearances. It is for these simulacra that man has always striven. And since freedom, as has been said, is no more than a *sensation*, what difference is there between being free and believing ourselves free?

*

Every action, as action, is possible only because we have broken with Paradise, whose memory, which poisons our hours, makes each of us a demoralized angel.

*

Our repressed prayers explode in sarcasms.

*

We have the feeling we are someone only when we brood over some misdeed.

*

If we make doubt a goal, it can be as comforting as faith. Doubt too is capable of fervor, doubt too, in its way, triumphs over every perplexity, doubt too has an answer to everything. How account for its bad reputation then? From the fact that it is rarer than faith, less accessible, and more mysterious. We cannot imagine what is going on in the doubter's house . . . .

*

In the marketplace, a five-year-old writhes, screams in a tantrum. Women rush to him, try to soothe him. He goes right on, exaggerates, exceeds all limits. The more you watch, the more you'd like to wring his neck. His mother, finally realizing he has to be taken away, implores the wild creature: "Come on, *darling*, let's go home now!" You think—with what satisfaction!—of Calvin, for whom children are "lumps of filth" or of Freud who labels them "polymorphous perverse." Either would certainly have said, "Suffer the little monsters to come unto me!"

*

In the decision to abjure salvation, there is no diabolic element; for if there were, what would account for the serenity which accompanies such a decision? Nothing diabolic induces serenity. In the Devil's vicinity, we are, on the contrary, morose—my case . . . . Hence my serenity is short-lived: just long enough to persuade me to have nothing to do with salavation. Luckily, I am often so persuaded, and each time, what peace!

*

To get up early, filled with energy and enthusiasm, wonderfully ready to commit some wretched nastiness.

*

"Free to the last degree"—this phrase raised the bum on the day he uttered it above philosophers, conquerors, and saints; for none of them, at the apex of his career, dared invoke such a success.

*

A fallen man is like all the rest of us except that he has not condescended to play the game. We reproach him for that, and avoid him, we resent his having revealed and displayed our secret—we rightly regard him as a wretch and a traitor.

*

Flung out of sleep by the question, "Where is *this* moment going?" "To death," was my answer, and I fell back asleep at once.

*

We should trust only explanations which invoke physiology and theology. Whatever happens between the two is of no importance.

*

Our pleasure in foreseeing a catastrophe diminishes as the catastrophe approaches and ceases altogether once it is upon us.

*

Wisdom disguises our wounds: it teaches us how to bleed in secret.

*

The critical moment for a prophet is the one when he is ultimately imbued by what he preaches, when he is conquered by his own vaticinations. Henceforth a slave, an automaton, he will occupy himself regretting the time when, a free man, he announced calamities without quite believing in them, when he fabricated fears for himself. It is not easy to act an Isaiah and a Jeremiah sincerely. Which is why most prophets *prefer* being impostors.

*

Everything that happens to us, everything that counts for us affords no interest for someone else: it is on the basis of this evidence that we should elaborate our rules of behavior. A reflective mind should banish from its intimate vocabulary the word *event*.

*

Anyone who hasn't died young *deserves* to die.

*

Nothing gives us a better conscience than to fall asleep with the clear view of one of our defects, which till then we hadn't dared admit, we hadn't even suspected.

*

Everything blurs and fades in human beings except the look in their eyes and the voice: without these, we could recognize no one after a few years.

*

At this very moment, almost everywhere, thousands and thousands are dying, while, clutching my pen, I vainly search for a word to annotate their agony.

*

To dwell on an action, however unmentionable, to invent scruples for yourself and get tangled in them, proves that you are still concerned with your kind, that you like to torment yourself on their account . . . . I shall consider myself liberated only on the day when, like murderers and sages, I have swept my conscience clean of all the impurities of remorse.

*

Tired of being myself—yet I keep praying the gods to restore me to myself.

*

To regret is to deliberate in the past tense—to substitute the possible for the irreparable, to cheat by heartbreak.

*

Delirium is incontestably finer than doubt, but doubt is *solider*.

*

Skepticism is the faith of what Montaigne calls undulant minds.

*

To see nothing but words in the calumny of words is the one way to endure that calumny without suffering. Dissect any remark made against yourself, isolate each syllable, treat it with the disdain an adjective is worth, a substantive, an adverb . . . . Or else liquidate the calumniator on the spot.

*

Our claims to detachment always help us not to ward off blows but to digest them. In any humiliation, there is a first and a second period. It is in the second that our coquetry with *sagesse* is revealed to be useful.

*

What place do we occupy in the "universe"? A point, if that! Why reproach ourselves when we are evidently so insignificant? Once we make this observation, we grow calm at once: henceforth, no more bother, no more frenzy, metaphysical or otherwise. And then that point dilates, swells, substitutes itself for space. And everything begins all over again.

*

To know is to discern the bearing of illusion, a key word as essential to the Vedanta as to the song, to the only ways of translating the experience of unreality.

*

In the British Museum, looking at the mummy of a singer whose tiny finger-nails stick out of the wrappings, I remember swearing never to say "I . . . " again.

*

There is only one sign that indicates we have understood everything: tears *without cause.*

*

Fear of an imminent collapse of the brain counts for a great deal in the need to pray.

*

Happiness and misery being evils for approximately the same reason, the one way of avoiding them is to make yourself external to everything.

*

When I spend days and days among texts concerned with nothing but serenity, contemplation, and ascesis, I am filled with a longing to rush out into the street and break the skull of the first person I meet.

*

The proof that this world is not a success is that we can compare ourselves without indecency to Him Who is supposed to have created it, but not to Napoleon or even to a bum, especially if the latter is incomparable of his kind.

*

"It could not have done better"—a remark made by a pagan about providence which no Father of the Church was honest enough to apply to God.

*

Speech and silence. We feel safer with a madman who talks than with one who cannot open his mouth.

*

If a Christian heresy—any one of them—had triumphed, it would not have wasted its time on nuances. Bolder than the Church, it would also have been more intolerant, since more convinced. No doubt about it: victorious, the Cathari would have outstripped the Inquisitors. For any victim, however noble, let us have a pity without illusions.

*

What remains of a philosopher is his temperament, what makes him *forget himself*, yield to his contradictions, his whims, reactions incompatible with the fundamental lines of his system. If he seeks truth, let him free himself of all concern with coherence. He must express only what he thinks and not what he had *decided* to think. The more alive he will be, the more he will let himself *be himself*; and will survive only if he takes no account of what he *ought* to think.

*

When we are to meditate upon vacuity, impermanence, nirvana, crouching or lying down is the best position. It is the one in which these themes were conceived. It is only in the West that man thinks *standing up*. Which accounts perhaps for the unfortunately positive character of our philosophy.

*

We can endure an affront only by imagining the *scenes* of revenge, of the triumph we shall someday have over the wretch who has flouted us. Without this prospect, we would fall victim to disturbances which would radically renew madness.

*

Every mortal agony is in itself curious; the most interesting, however, remains that of the cynic, of the man who *theoretically* disdains it.

*

What is the name of this bone I am touching? What can it have in common with *me*? I should begin the operation all over again with another part of my body and continue until the moment when nothing is *mine*.

*

To have both the taste for provocation and the taste for

effacement—to be by instinct a spoilsport and by conviction a corpse!

*

After so many living men, *all* dead—how tiring to die in our turn and to suffer, like them, this inept fear! How explain that it still persists, that it is not exhausted or discredited, and that we can still sustain it as intensely as the first mortal?

*

The hermit assumes responsibilities only toward himself or toward everyone; in no case toward *someone*. He takes refuge in solitude in order to have no one in his care: himself and the universe—enough.

*

If I were sure of my indifference to salvation, I should be far and away the happiest man who ever lived.

*

To come to your senses, there is nothing like being "forgotten." No one coming between us and what counts. The more others turn away from us, the more they labor toward our perfection: they save us by abandoning us.

*

My doubts about Providence never last long: Who, except for Providence, would be in a position to distribute so punctually our ration of daily defeats?

*

"Take nothing to heart," murmurs the man who blames himself each time he suffers, and who loses no opportunity for suffering.

*

The battle waged in each individual by the fanatic and the impostor is the reason we never know *whom* to turn to.

*

"What are you working on? What are you doing now?" Would anyone have dared ask Pyrrho or Laotsŭ such a question? We do not imagine that the questions no one could have asked our idols can be asked of us.

*

By nature I am so refractory to the slightest undertaking that to bring myself to perform one I first have to read some biography of Alexander or Genghis Khan.

*

What should make old age endurable is the pleasure of seeing disappear, one by one, all those who have believed in us and whom we can no longer disappoint.

*

It is my delight to gloss our fall from grace—I love living as a parasite of original sin.

*

If we could make ourselves *inhumiliable!*

*

Contrary to the common allegation, suffering attaches, rivets, us to life: it is *our* suffering, we are flattered to be able to endure it, it testifies to our quality as a being and not as a specter. So virulent is the pride of suffering that it is exceeded only by the pride of having suffered.

*

Determined to save the past, regret represents our sole recourse against the maneuvers of forgetting: What is regret in substance, if not memory on the offensive? By resuscitating so many episodes and distorting them at will, it offers us all the versions we want of our life, so that it is correct to assert that it is thanks to regret that our life seems to us at once pitiable and fulfilled.

*

Every theoretical formula, appearing in sleep, interrupts its course. Dreams are events. Once one of them turns into a *problem*, or ends in a discovery, we waken with a start. "To think" asleep is an anomaly, frequent among the oppressed, among those who in fact sleep badly, because their miseries culminate in definitions, night after night.

*

We make martyrs of ourselves, we create, by torments, a "conscience"; and then, we realize with horror that we can never get rid of it again.

*

The discomfort that follows on a pettiness is the state most favorable to self-examination; it even identifies itself with such reflections. Scarcely surprising that each time it seizes upon us, we should have the impression of knowing ourselves at last.

*

The only subversive mind is the one which questions the obligation to exist; all the others, the anarchist at the head of the list, compromise with the established order.

*

My preferences: the age of the Cave Man, the century of the Enlightenment. But I do not forget that the caves opened onto history, and the salons onto the guillotine.

*

Everywhere, flesh for money. But what can a subsidized flesh be worth? In the old days we engendered out of conviction or by accident; today, in order to gain a subsistance allowance or a tax deduction. Such excess of calculation cannot fail to damage the quality of the spermatozoa.

*

To look for a meaning in anything is less the act of a naif than of a masochist.

*

To become conscious of our complete, our radical destructibility is salvation itself. But it is to go counter to our deepest tendencies to know we are, at every moment, destructible. Might salvation be an exploit *contra naturam?*

*

Frivolous, disconnected, an amateur at everything, I shall have known thoroughly only the disadvantage of having been born.

*

We should philosophize as if "philosophy" didn't exist, like some troglodyte dazed or daunted by the procession of scourges which pass before his eyes.

*

To relish one's pain—the feeling and even the expression figure in Homer, though of course as an exception. As a general rule, we must wait till more recent times for it. It is a long road from the epic to the diary.

*

We would not be interested in human beings if we did not have the hope of someday meeting someone worse off than ourselves.

*

Rats, confined in a limited space and fed solely on those chemical products we stuff them with become, apparently, much nastier and more aggressive than usual. Doomed as they multiply to pile on top of each other, men will detest each other much more than before, they will even invent unwonted forms of hatred, they will rend each other as they never did before, and a universal civil war will explode, not because of claims but because of humanity's inability to witness the spectacle it affords itself. Even now, if for a single moment it glimpsed the *whole* future, humanity would not survive that moment.

*

The only true solitude is where we brood upon the urgency of a prayer—a prayer *posterior* to God and to faith itself.

*

We should keep reminding ourselves that everything that delights or distresses us corresponds to nothing, that it is all quite meaningless and futile . . . . Well, I keep reminding myself of it every day, and I continue nonetheless in my delight, in my distress.

*

We are all deep in a hell each moment of which is a miracle.